THREE COMEDIES

THE DRAMA LIBRARY

General Editor: Edward Thompson

Noah	André Obey
The Importance of Being Earnest	Oscar Wilde
Time and the Conways	J. B. Priestley
Ten Diminutive Dramas	Maurice Baring
Hassan	J. E. Flecker
The Government Inspector	Nikolai Gogol
A Month in the Country	Ivan Turgenev
Cyrano de Bergerac	Edmond Rostand
An Enemy of the People	Henrik Ibsen
Three Medieval Plays	*Edited:* John Allen
The Snow Queen	Suria Magito and Rudolf Weil
The Satire of the Three Estates	Sir David Lindsay
Tamburlaine the Great	Christopher Marlowe
Emmanuel	James Forsyth
Like Stars Appearing	Viscount Duncannon
The Makers of Violence	Robert Gittings
His Eminence of England	Hugh Ross Williamson
Two Saints' Plays	Leo Lehman: Robert Gittings
The Player King	Christopher Hassall
Will Shakespeare	Clemence Dane
Spring, 1600	Emlyn Williams
Trespass	Emlyn Williams
Cavalcade	Noël Coward
Letter from Paris	Dodie Smith
Carrington, V.C.	Dorothy and Campbell Christie
Six Characters in Search of an Author	Luigi Pirandello
Four One-Act Plays	Tyrone Guthrie: Robert Kemp John Allen: Robert Gittings
Second Book of One-Act Plays	Emlyn Williams Hubert Nicholson: Kenneth Lillington: H. F. Rubenstein
Good Friday	John Masefield
The Living Room	Graham Greene
Dark of the Moon	Richardson and Berney
The Wind of Heaven	Emlyn Williams
Out of This Wood	Robert Gittings
I Capture the Castle	Dodie Smith
The Teahouse of the August Moon	John Patrick
Sabrina Fair	Samuel Taylor
Someone Waiting	Emlyn Williams
The Light of Heart	Emlyn Williams
The Corn is Green	Emlyn Williams
The Chester Mystery Plays	*Edited:* Maurice Hussey
Hotel Paradiso	Feydeau and Desvallières
The Wild Duck	Henrik Ibsen
Three Comedies	Ludvig Holberg

THREE COMEDIES

by

LUDVIG HOLBERG

THE TRANSFORMED PEASANT
THE ARABIAN POWDER
THE HEALING SPRING

English Text and Introduction
by

REGINALD SPINK

WILLIAM HEINEMANN LTD
MELBOURNE :: LONDON :: TORONTO

FIRST PUBLISHED 1957

PUBLISHED BY
WILLIAM HEINEMANN LTD.
99 GREAT RUSSELL STREET, LONDON, W.C.1.
PRINTED IN GREAT BRITAIN FOR THE PUBLISHERS BY
J. AND J. GRAY, EDINBURGH

CONTENTS

INTRODUCTION

by

REGINALD SPINK

LUDVIG HOLBERG, " the Molière of the North ", was born at Bergen in 1684, the son of a lieutenant-colonel. After matriculating at the University of Copenhagen, capital of the dual kingdom of Denmark–Norway, he spent twelve years travelling around western Europe, mostly on foot, studying at the leading centres of learning and getting a living by teaching music and languages. At Oxford, where he stayed from 1706 to 1708, he was hospitably entertained by the students of Magdalen College in particular, who enjoyed his flute-playing and his witty conversation. He afterwards settled in Copenhagen, where eventually he became Professor of History and established a European reputation as a moral philosopher and historian. In 1747 he was created a Baron. He died in Copenhagen in 1754.

A small, almost diminutive man with delicate features, and of delicate health, Holberg was highly strung and rather aloof. He had few close friends and he never married; the considerable fortune which he amassed by shrewd investment coupled with frugality bordering on miserliness he left to the principal Danish public school. As warmth of personality radiates from his works, the aloofness must have sprung from his extreme sensitiveness. A remarkable blend of artist and scholar, he combined lucid intellect and biting wit with good-humoured tolerance, and he detested affectation, dogma, and all forms of systematic philosophizing. The range of his mind is impressive: besides thirty-three plays, he wrote a treatise on law, a history of Europe, and the first attempted history of the world; he introduced into Scandinavia the literary essay on the lines of the *Spectator*, in which, in serious and mock-serious vein, he discoursed on almost every topic under the sun, from books and women to taxes and tobacco; and he wrote satirical works both in prose after the manner of Swift and in verse. He has been called "the founder of Danish literature", and the Danes know him affectionately as "Father Holberg".

The meaning of this is appreciated when one knows that the speech of the Danish Court and polite society in his day was German (as in Germany it was French!), that most Danish authors wrote in German or Latin, and that until the first truly national theatre opened in 1722, with a performance of a translation of Molière's *L'Avare*, German or French was the stage language. Latin was still the *lingua franca* of scholars, and Holberg himself wrote scholarly works in that language. But he turned to Danish for his plays, the first fifteen of which were produced in rapid succession soon after the Molière translation and at the same theatre. Holberg, as he freely admitted, owed much to Molière as well as to the Commedia dell'Arte, but the action of his plays usually takes place on a lower social level. Perhaps he owed still more to Plautus, the Roman comedy-writer, whom he greatly admired.

Holberg's masterpieces are *The Political Tinker*, *Erasmus Montanus*, and *Jeppe on the Hill*, the last of which is included in this selection under its more pregnant sub-title, *The Transformed Peasant*. Like most of his plays, it is a satirical comedy, the butt in this case being the ignorant peasant of the period. The Danish peasants of Holberg's time were a backward and poverty-ridden class, subject to crippling taxes and labour services which made them little better than serfs. But the first stirrings of their struggle for liberty were beginning to be felt and, after an initial setback, they were eventually emancipated in 1788. The play might lead one to suppose that Holberg was not on the side of the angels in this matter, but in fact he supported reforms under the enlightened Autocracy and was a benevolent landlord in his dealings with the peasants on his own estate.

The other plays in this selection are one-acters and were partly chosen for that reason, because of a presumed demand for one-act plays among serious amateurs. In *The Arabian Powder*, another social satire, we find Holberg directing the shafts of his wit at the contemporary folly of alchemy and seizing the opportunity to get in some well-aimed digs at social snobbery. *The Healing Spring*, on the other hand, is a pure comedy of intrigue of a type which derives from Plautus and Terence, and their Greek model Menander, *via* the Commedia dell'Arte. The characters are the stock figures—the heavy father, the scheming lovers, and the clever servants—and the play is compounded of the traditional ingredients of impersonation, unmasking, and sudden recognition, the situations being nevertheless well contrived and the conventions employed with grace and charm. It is an interesting detail that the servants of these and most of Holberg's plays bear the same names, Henrik having been the real name of the first impersonator of the man-servants.

All three plays were first performed in Copenhagen in the 1720s, when Holberg was about forty. *The Healing Spring* appears in English translation for the first time.

Though in many respects so English in outlook, Ludvig Holberg has been singularly neglected in this country. In France, in Holland, in Germany, and in Russia his reputation has stood high. Edmund Gosse called him " the first writer in Europe during his generation ". Yet most of his plays (and most of his other works) have never been translated. Sadder still, those which have appeared have hardly ever been performed. Can it be that the approach has been too academic, that translators have concentrated on verbal accuracy and scholarliness, on the word rather than the spirit and the savour of the works? It is a disastrous policy where plays are concerned.

Holberg wrote in a colloquial idiom and no professor was ever less academic. But the idiom has become archaic, so that a literal translation or pastiche is bound to lose the vigour and the freshness of the original, and to an audience unschooled in the Holberg tradition may be only half intelligible. In communion with the spirit of Holberg, therefore, I have put the plays into plain modern English, while avoiding, I hope, incongruous modern slang. In order to facilitate the presentation of this classic playwright on a stage all too long unfamiliar with him I have also made a number of minor adjustments. A few examples will illustrate the method.

In *The Transformed Peasant* and *The Arabian Powder*, in particular, I have condensed long opening monologues and duologues, and in the former play I have brought the Curtain down rather earlier than Holberg and omitted the moralizing epilogue. On the original title-page this play is described as a " Comedy in Five Acts " (though there are more than five scenes). To conform to current fashion, I have turned it into a three-act play by the simple device of linking the second and third acts, which are practically continuous, and then combining the remaining scenes to form Act Three, scenes one, two, and three. In *The Arabian Powder* I have made a few minor adjustments in order to avoid awkward changes of sets, a matter which they ordered more casually in Holberg's day, and I have followed a similar procedure in the Prologue to *The Healing Spring* (which is not so called by the author). Holberg rather extravagantly terms this play a " Comedy in Three Acts ", on the strength of an elaborate scenic interlude between the two parts of the play proper. This is intended to show crowds travelling to the spring; and as it is pure spectacle, difficult to stage, I have omitted it. The original title of this play defies neat translation, but means something like " The Journey to the Spring ". In the two short plays I have " anglicized " some of the names in order to ensure correct pronunciation without recourse to notes (*e.g.*, "Pernilla " for "Pernille ", " Hieronimus " for " Jeronimus "). In all three plays I have expanded the stage directions and added new ones as seemed necessary or desirable. Apart from these minor adaptations, the plays—in plot, characters, and general dramatic sequence—are all Holberg's.

When I censure the follies of men, I am mindful of my own; when I laugh at others I laugh at myself.

Holberg: *Epistles*

THE TRANSFORMED PEASANT

(Jeppe paa Bjerget eller Den forvandlede Bonde)

A COMEDY IN THREE ACTS

1723

CHARACTERS

JEPPE, a peasant
NILLE, his wife
JACOB, an innkeeper
BARON
SECRETARY
VALET
ERIC, a footman
FIRST DOCTOR
SECOND DOCTOR
BAILIFF
BAILIFF'S WIFE
FIRST WATCHMAN
SECOND WATCHMAN
COUNSEL for the Prosecution
COUNSEL for the Defence
FOOTMEN, USHERS

ACT ONE: Outside Jeppe's Cottage

ACT TWO: A Room at the Manor

ACT THREE: Scene One: Outside Jeppe's Cottage
Scene Two: A Court of Law
Scene Three: Outside Jeppe's Cottage

TIME: About 1720

PLACE: Denmark

NOTE ON PRONUNCIATION: JEPPE *pronounced* YEPPER; NILLE *pronounced* NILLER; JACOB *pronounced* YACKOB.

THE TRANSFORMED PEASANT

Act One

A country scene in Denmark, about 1720. *On the right is a peasant's cottage; on the extreme left, the entrance to an inn.* Nille, *a peasant woman, is scrubbing the cottage step.*

Nille: I never saw such a lazy scoundrel as that husband of mine! The idle wretch! It's all I can do to get him out of bed in a morning, and even then I have to drag him out by the scruff of his neck. There he was, snoring away fit to blow the roof off, for all he knows it's market-day! And then the parson says I'm too hard on him! "Nille," he says, "he's the master, you know, by rights." Master! Him master! "Pastor," I says, "make him master in my house and there'll be no more rent for the landlord—let alone tithes for you. "Why, he'd job the lot of us away for gin, himself and all," I says. That shut *him* up. The bailiff now, he agrees with *me*. "Don't you take any notice of the rector," he says. "It's all very well him talking," he says; "the prayer book tells you to love, honour, and obey your husband, but your farm contract says you've to look after your farm and pay your dues—and it's newer than the prayer book. If Jeppe won't work, you give him what for, Nille," he says. Well, now, I got the idle villain out of bed all right. But when I go back to see how he's getting on, bless me if he isn't sitting on a chair fast asleep, with one leg in his breeches and the other out! But I know one thing he's got respect for, and that's Master Eric, my stick! (*Shouting into the house.*) Hi, Jeppe, haven't you got your clothes on yet? You'd better shift yourself, unless you want another taste of Master Eric! Come on, now!

Jeppe (*appearing at a window*): Give me time to finish dressing, Nille. I can't go to market without my coat and breeches on, can I?

NILLE: You've had time to get ten pairs of breeches on since I woke you up.

JEPPE: Have you put Master Eric away, Nille?

NILLE: Yes, but I know where to find him again if you don't look sharp. Come on, now, stir yourself! (*Enter* JEPPE.) Just look at the slow-coach! Put a jerk into yourself, you dawdler! Get yourself off to the market and fetch me seven pounds of soft soap. Here's the money. And see that you're back within four hours from now, or you'll have Master Eric dancing a jig on your backside. So the sooner you get started, the better!

JEPPE: How do you expect me to walk eighteen miles in four hours, Nille?

NILLE: Walk? Who said you'd to walk, you cuckoo? You're to run! Go on! Off you go! (*And with this she goes indoors.*)

JEPPE: Ay, there she goes—in to her breakfast! And what do I get! Nothing! Not a blessed bite! Eighteen miles on an empty stomach! It's a damned shame! Wife? The cat! And then they say Jeppe drinks! But they don't say why Jeppe drinks! What man wouldn't? With a wife to beat him like a dog, a bailiff to drive him till he nearly drops, and a parish clerk always making a cuckold of him! It's all very well for neighbour Christopher to say I should take her in hand and teach her a lesson, but he doesn't know Nille. Has his wife got a Master Eric under the bed? No! If she had, he'd sing a different tune! Oh, what a thirst I've got! I could drink a bucketful! I shall have to wet my whistle before I start. I wonder if Jacob'll let me have a drop on tick. No harm in asking. A man can't go eighteen miles without a drop of nourishment. (*He knocks at the inn door.*) Hi, Jacob! Hullo, there! Are you up, Jacob? Open the door there, Jacob, old man!

JACOB (*appearing at the door in his shirt and trousers*): Hullo, who's there?

JEPPE: Me, Jacob! How are you?

JACOB: Oh, it's you, is it? What's brought *you* at this time of morning?

JEPPE: A thirst, Jacob! Give us a glass o' gin.

JACOB: Where's your money?

JEPPE: I'll pay you tomorrow, Jacob.

JACOB: Won't do! No credit allowed at this house. I've told you that before. And don't come telling me you've no money, because I don't believe it.

JEPPE: It's the honest truth, Jacob.

JACOB: None at all?

JEPPE: No, none at all. Except some of the wife's I've got to go to market with.

JACOB: That'll do. What are you worrying about? You can always beat 'em down at the market. What have you got to buy with it?

JEPPE: Soft soap.

JACOB: All right. Tell her it's gone up.

JEPPE: That's all very well, Jacob, but she might find out. I know what that would mean. (*He ruefully feels his back.*) I can feel it already.

JACOB: Rubbish! How could she find out? You just swear you spent the lot. I'm surprised at you, Jeppe. I thought you'd more sense.

JEPPE: Mebbe you're right, Jacob. I might do that.

JACOB: Give us your money, then.

JEPPE: All right, then. Here you are. But I want some change, mind you!

JACOB *takes* JEPPE'S *money and goes in, returning immediately with a large glass. He takes a pull at it himself before handing it to* JEPPE.

JACOB: Your health, Jeppe!

JEPPE: You took a good nip there, didn't you?

JACOB: What are you grumbling about? It's usual to drink a customer's health, isn't it?

JEPPE: Yes, but he was a damned thieving rogue that started the custom. Good health, Jacob!

JACOB: It'll do you good, that.

JEPPE: Ah, that's grand. I feel better already.

JACOB: Have another, Jeppe. I haven't any change, so you'll have to. Unless I owe you one till you come back. I'm right out of small change this morning.

JEPPE: What! You dirty cheat, you! Oh, all right, then, damn you! I may as well have it now as later. A gin in the belly's worth two on the shelf! (*He laughs at his joke.*) But if you half empty it again, I warn you you'll get no more money out o' me.

JACOB *replenishes the glass.*

JACOB (*drinking as before*): Your health, Jeppe!

JEPPE (*taking the glass and emptying it at a gulp*): Good health! And good riddance to all wives, is what I say! Ah, I feel a lot better for that! It's warmed me up right down here! (*He rubs his stomach.*)

JACOB: Good luck, Jeppe!

JEPPE: Thanks, Jacob.

JACOB *goes in, shutting the door after him.* JEPPE, *the gin beginning to take effect, starts to sing.*

Oh, a little black hen and a brown one, too,
Once set their caps at a cock-a-doodle-doo.

I could do with another drink! I'm dying for another drink! And, what's more, I'm going to have another drink! No, Jeppe, better not. Only cause trouble. Damn it, if I could get away from this place I'd be all right! But something seems to be holding me back. I shall have to have another! Now, Jeppe, be careful. Remember Nille—with Master Eric in her hand! Ooh!! It's no use, I can't help it! I've got to have another! You see, it's like this. My belly says " Yes ", but my backside says " No ". They can't both be right! Which am I to listen to? (*Holding himself in front with one hand and behind with the other.*) Seein' that my belly's nearer to me than my backside, I'm going to try that first. I'm going to knock. Ooh, there's that woman again! God help me, what am I to do? Now, now, Jeppe, control yourself! Shame on you, Jeppe, to start a row for a glass of gin! No! No, I won't! Not this time, I won't! Oh, but I'm thirsty!! If only I hadn't had that first one I should have been all right! Now I'm lost! Damn you, legs! Go, damn you!! They won't. They won't! They're off back again! I'm a civil war! My belly pulls me one way and my backside the other! Go, you dogs, I say! You mangy beasts, you, go! The devil they will! They're off back to Jacob's again. Getting my old nag out of the stable's nothing to this! Oh, I could do with a drink! He'll have to give me one on tick this time. (*Knocking at the door.*) Hi, there, Jacob! Another glass of gin, Jacob!

JACOB (*opening the door*): What, you back again! I might have known you hadn't had enough! What's a glass of gin to a tippler like you? It only gives you a thirst.

JEPPE: That's right, Jacob. You hit it. Give me another glass. (*As* JACOB *goes to get it.*) He'll have to allow me credit this time, whether he likes it or not.

JACOB (*returning with the glass*): Here you are, then, Jeppe. Money first, though.

JEPPE: No, gin first.

JACOB: Money first, or you'll not get a drop! No credit allowed in this house! I've told you before!

JEPPE (*almost in tears*): Let me owe you for this one, Jacob. Just this once, Jacob! You know me. I'm an honest man.

JACOB: No credit.

JEPPE: All right, then, you miserable skinflint, there's your money! Take it and give me the gin!

He hands over the money. JACOB *takes a swig at the glass as before, and hands it to* JEPPE.

JACOB: Your health, Jeppe!

JEPPE (*draining the glass*): Ah, Ah, I feel better for that!!

JACOB: That should keep your inside warm and moist for a bit.

JEPPE: The great thing about gin is that it puts heart into a man. It's wonderful the way that last glass has made me forget my troubles. Who's afraid of Master Eric now? What do you think of this, Jacob? (*Singing.*)

There was a little man and he had a little wife,
And her name was Nille Berg, Berg, Berg.
She threatened to wallop him with Master Eric,
But he walloped her instead, instead.

I made that one up myself, Jacob.

JACOB: H'm, sounded like it!

JEPPE: I'm not such a fool as you might think, you know. I've another one I've made up about a cobbler. It goes like this:

The cobbler took his fiddle and bow, tra-la-la, tra-la-la.

JACOB: You fool! You mean fiddler!

JEPPE: Eh? Fiddler? Fiddler, you say? Oh, fiddler! Another gin, Jacob!

JACOB: Your money?

JEPPE (*producing a coin*): Here! Surprised you, didn't it?

JACOB: Right! (*He goes to get the gin. Meanwhile* JEPPE *sings :*)

JEPPE:
Oh, the earth drinks the rain,
The sea drinks the sun,
And the sun drinks the sea.
If the whole world drinks,
Then why not me?

JACOB (*returning and drinking first as before*): Your health, Jeppe!

JEPPE: And yours, Jacob!

JACOB: And to the devil with all wives, I say!

JEPPE: *Ick dank* you, Jacob!

JACOB: Didn't know you spoke German!

JEPPE: *Ja*; Only when I'm—I'm—drunk!

JACOB: That's at least once a day!

JEPPE: Oh, yes, I'm a man for languages, I am. Ten years in the militia, you know. *Ick bin, du bist, er ist*——

JACOB: I know. Didn't we serve two years in the same company?

JEPPE: That's right, comrade. Remember that time they hanged you? Oh, that was a day! The day you deserted!

JACOB: The day they were going to hang me, you mean. They let me off. A miss is as good as a mile!

JEPPE: Remember that auction on the heath? That was an auction, that was! You know the one I mean!

JACOB: Ah, what don't I remember!

JEPPE: I'll never forget the enemy's first valley that day! Must have killed off 3,000 men! Say 4,000! Something like that! Ah, that was a day, Jacob. *Kannst du das* remember? *Was*? I'll not deny I was scared that day.

JACOB: Ah, yes. Puts the fear of God into you, it does.

JEPPE: The night before that auction I remember I sat up all night, reading David's palms.

JACOB: You know, Jeppe, I can't understand why you let that old woman o' yours bully you as she does. You—an old soldier!

JEPPE: Bully me! Bully me!! I wish I had her here! I'd soon

show her!! Another glass, Jacob! I still have a bit left. When that's gone, you'll have to give me credit. And, Jacob, bring a tankard of ale while you're there. (*While* JACOB *is getting the drinks* JEPPE *sings again* :)

In Leipzig once there lived a man,
In Leipzig once there lived a man,
In Leipzig once there lived a man, tra-la,
And he married a pretty wife.

JACOB *returns with a glass and a tankard, and, as before, takes a drink from both before handing them to* JEPPE.

JACOB: Your health, Jeppe!

JEPPE (*drinking alternately from glass and tankard*): Good health, Jacob! To the devil with Nille! To the devil with Master Eric! I'm my own master, I am! I'll please myself and drink when I like! Here's to everybody! Hurray—hic!!

JACOB: Good health to the bailiff, Jeppe!

JEPPE: To the bailiff! For he's a jolly good fellow!! He's a gentleman, the bailiff! Stand him a drink and he'll see you all right with the landlord. Tickle his palm, and he'll swear black's white that you can't pay your rent! Jacob, I'm th-thirsty! Give us another! I'll see you get your money. What's wrong with my credit, Jacob?

JACOB: No, Jeppe, you've had all that's good for you. I don't believe in letting my customers get drunk. I'd rather lose my licence.

JEPPE: Just one, Jacob.

JACOB: No, Jeppe, no more this time. You've a long way to go.

JEPPE: Dog! Beast! Rogue! Hic-c!

JACOB: See you when you come back. (*And he goes in and shuts the door.*)

JEPPE: Jep-Jeppe, you're—dr-drunk! Who says I'm drunk? I'm not drunk! Yes, you are, I say! Your legs won't carry you! Yes, they will! Stand up, you dogs! Ah, that's better! I—wonder what time it is! (*Thumping on the door.*) Hi, you, Jacob, come out, you cur! Give me another drink, I say! Stand up, you dogs! The devil they will! (*Imagining he is drinking.*) Thank you, Jacob! And now another one. Your health! (*Fancying he sees somebody passing.*) I say, you! Which is the right way to the market, eh? Stand up, there, I say! He's dr-drunk! Jeppe, you've been drinking. You drank like a fish! You're drunk, I say! Dead drunk! Drunk as a lord! Drunk as a—a lord!!

Muttering " Drunk as a lord ", he staggers and falls on to a dung-hill, and is soon snoring heavily. After a while, the BARON *enters with his* SECRETARY, *his* VALET, *the* FOOTMAN ERIC *and another* FOOTMAN.

BARON: Yes, there's every sign of a good harvest this year. The barley especially is looking well.

SECRETARY: Indeed it is, my lord. But I'm afraid it means that a bushel of corn isn't likely to fetch much more than five marks.

BARON: Still, in a good year the peasants can't help but be better off than in a bad one, whatever the prices.

SECRETARY: I don't know about that, my lord. In any case, they'll always complain and always come begging for seed grain, good year or bad. The more they have, the more they drink. Now this innkeeper here—he's a fellow who works hard to keep the peasants poor. They even say he salts the drinks to make his customers more thirsty.

BARON: Dreadful! We must get rid of the fellow. But what on earth is that? A body? You hear of nothing but accidents these days. One of you go and see what it is.

ERIC: It's Jeppe Berg, the man with the shrewish wife. Hullo, there, Jeppe! Wake up, Jeppe! I can't wake him, my lord! He's dead drunk.

BARON: Leave him, then. And yet I'd love to teach him a lesson. Now, my men, listen to me. You're usually so full of ideas. Can't one of you think of a good joke to play off on him?

SECRETARY: Why don't we put a halter round his neck to frighten him? Or we might shave his hair off.

VALET: I suggest we blacken his face, my lord. And lie in wait to see what happens when he goes home to his wife.

BARON: All right! But I wager Eric knows of something better. What do you say, Eric?

ERIC: I have a good idea, if you agree to it, my lord.

BARON: What is it?

ERIC: To transform him.

ALL: To what?

ERIC: Transform him. Promote him into baron in your place and then drop him down again with a bump. That should teach him a lesson.

BARON: And how would you go about it?

ERIC: Take him home, undress him, and put him in your lordship's best bed. When he wakes up we'll all pretend he's you, and he won't know whether he's awake or dreaming.

BARON: And what next?

ERIC: Then when we've persuaded him that he really is the baron, we'll get him drunk again, put his old clothes on him, and leave him where we found him. That's my proposal.

BARON: And a very good one, too, Eric. But suppose he wakes up before we can carry out this brilliant idea of yours?

ERIC: He won't do that, my lord. When Jeppe Berg's drunk he's one of the soundest sleepers in Christendom.

VALET: That's right, my lord. I remember we once fixed some rockets to his coat-collar. Did that wake him? Not a bit! When they'd gone off he was snoring away as peacefully as ever.

BARON: Right! We'll do it. Take him away, wash him, dress him in a linen shirt, and put him to sleep it off in my best bed. We'll both teach him a lesson and have a good day's sport out of this!

Amid much amusement, they carry JEPPE *off, and the* CURTAIN *falls.*

ACT TWO

A room at the Manor. JEPPE *is asleep in the Baron's bed. Hanging over a chair at the bedside is a gold-brocaded dressing-gown.* JEPPE *wakes and rubs his eyes. He looks round in bewilderment, rubs his eyes again, and, putting his hand to his head, pulls off a gold-brocaded night-cap. He spits on his fingers and rubs his eyes again. Then he turns the cap over in his hands and stares at his linen shirt, at the dressing-gown, and at the room in amazement. As soft music begins to play* JEPPE *wrings his hands and finally bursts into tears. Gradually he stops weeping and the music also ceases.*

JEPPE: Eh? Eh? What's this? I must be dreaming! Where am I? (*Calling in a subdued and scared voice.*) Nille, Nille, Nille! Nille, I—I think I'm in Heaven! Me! Me, in Heaven!! No, it can't be me! I can still feel my aching bones, though. It seems to be my voice; and this is my own hollow tooth. It seems to be me all right. But look at this night-cap! And this shirt! And all these other grand things!! And the music!! No, it can't be me!! I must be dreaming!! I'll pinch myself. (*He does.*) Ow! I'm awake all right! No, I don't believe it; I'm asleep! I'll wait till I wake up again! (*He lies down, but the music strikes up again and he sits up and bursts into tears.*) It can't be a dream! And I really seem to be me! Now, let's see. I'm Jeppe Berg, son of Niels Berg; my wife's called Nille and her stick's Master Eric; and I have three sons—Hans, Christopher, and Niels. This must be Heaven! I know—I've drunk myself to death! Doesn't seem to be so bad, though! I never felt a thing! And to think that Pastor Jesper's very likely preaching over me at this minute! He'd be surprised to know I'm here! Better than running eighteen miles for soft soap, this is! And being walloped with Master Eric and cuckolded by the parish clerk! But I'm thirsty, though! I'd give anything for a tankard of ale to wet my whistle with! What sense is there in all this finery, if I'm to die of thirst again? What was it the parson used to say? " And there shall be no more hunger or thirst." That's all he knows!! I'm fair dying of thirst!! No, this can't be heaven! I'm dreaming! Or else I'm drunk! Unless (*a light seems to dawn on him*)—unless I'm mad!! Oh! Oh! Oh! Help! Help!! Help!!!

The VALET *and the* TWO FOOTMEN, *who have been watching him from behind doors and curtains and have had great difficulty in containing themselves, enter at his cry.*

VALET: Good morning, my lord! Here is your lordship's dressing-gown, if it pleases your lordship to rise. Eric, fetch a towel and the water-basin. (*Eric goes.*)

JEPPE: Ah, good Master Valet, I'll get up. You're not going to do anything to me, are you?

VALET: Do anything to your lordship? Nobody would dream of doing anything to your lordship!

JEPPE: Tell me who I am before you do me in!

VALET: "Do you in?" Whatever can your lordship mean? Does your lordship mean to say that your lordship doesn't know who your lordship is?

JEPPE: I was Jeppe Berg yesterday. I'm blessed if I know who I am today.

VALET: It is a pleasure to see your lordship in such good spirits, and to find that it pleases your lordship to jest. But surely your lordship isn't weeping?

JEPPE (*blubbering*): I'm not your lordship! I swear I'm not! I'm only Jeppe Berg, one of the Baron's peasants. Send for my wife, Nille. She'll soon tell you. Only don't let her bring Master Eric with her!

VALET: This is all very strange! I can't understand it! Your lordship must be dreaming! Your lordship doesn't usually jest like this!

JEPPE: I don't know about dreaming! But I know I'm one of the Baron's peasants. My name's Jeppe Berg, and I've never been a lord or a baron in my life.

VALET (*to* ERIC, *who has returned with the towel and basin*): What can this mean, Eric? I'm afraid his lordship isn't feeling well today.

ERIC: Perhaps his lordship isn't fully awake yet. Do you think he has been talking in his sleep?

VALET: No, Eric, his lordship seems to be under some sort of delusion. Perhaps we had better send for his doctors. Will you call them, Eric?

ERIC: I'll fetch them straight away. (*Exit.*)

VALET: Your lordship must get these strange ideas out of your lordship's head. Your lordship is frightening the whole household. Don't you know me, your lordship?

JEPPE: How should I? I don't even know myself.

VALET: Can this be possible? Fancy your lordship talking like this. And fancy your lordship being in such a state!! Surely your lordship can remember what your lordship did yesterday? When your lordship was out shooting?

JEPPE: Shooting! I've never been shooting! I never poached a rabbit in my life!!

VALET: But, your lordship, I was with you all day yesterday.

JEPPE: No! I was at Jacob's yesterday. Drinking gin all day. How could I have gone shooting?

VALET: Oh, your lordship, stop saying such things. I beg you on my knees. (*To* ERIC, *who has returned.*) Did you send for the doctors, Eric?

ERIC: Yes, they'll be here directly.

VALET: Let's help his lordship into his dressing-gown. Perhaps a walk in the fresh air would do him good. Will it please your lordship to put your dressing-gown on?

JEPPE: All right. Do what you like with me, so long as you don't do me in. I've done no harm. I only liked a drink now and then.

JEPPE *has got out of bed, and they are helping him on with the dressing-gown when the* TWO DOCTORS *arrive.*

Good morning, your lordship!

1ST DOCTOR: We regret to hear that your lordship is not feeling well.

VALET: Alas, Doctor, I'm afraid his lordship must be very ill!

2ND DOCTOR: How does your lordship feel now?

JEPPE: Not so bad now. Only a bit thirsty after all that gin I had. Give me a tankard of ale and leave me in peace. That's all the medicine I want.

1ST DOCTOR (*to* 2ND DOCTOR): He seems to be wandering in his mind, Doctor.

2ND DOCTOR: The worse he is, the quicker it should run its course. Will your lordship allow me to feel your pulse? (*To* 1ST DOCTOR.) What do you think, Doctor?

1ST DOCTOR: Immediate bleeding is the remedy I prescribe.

2ND DOCTOR: I disagree, Doctor. I think other methods are called for in a case like this. Clearly, a nightmare must have unbalanced his lordship's mind, so he imagines himself to be a peasant. He must be entertained with his favourite pastimes. I prescribe a good meal and plenty to drink. Meanwhile, let his favourite music be played to him. (*Mysteriously, gay music strikes up.*)

VALET: Isn't that your lordship's favourite piece?

JEPPE: Eh? Oh, anything you like. I say, do you always have such goings-on here?

VALET: As often as it pleases your lordship. Your lordship pays for it.

JEPPE: It's the first I've heard of it.

1ST DOCTOR: The effect of the sickness, my lord. One forgets the past. I once had a patient who was much worse. After drinking heavily for two days he could remember nothing at all. He even believed he had lost his head.

JEPPE: It's the other way round with our parson. He thinks he's got a head and hasn't. (*There is general laughter at this quip.*)

2ND DOCTOR: It's encouraging to hear your lordship jest. That's a good sign. But to return to my story. This patient of mine used to walk round the town asking if anybody had found his head. But he recovered in the end; and now he's a parish clerk in Jutland.

JEPPE: He wouldn't need a head for that. (*Renewed laughter.*)

1ST DOCTOR (*to* 2ND DOCTOR): I wonder, Doctor, if you remember that case, some years ago, of the man who believed his head was full of flies. They just couldn't disillusion him. Then, finally, a very sensible doctor succeeded in curing him. He poulticed his head with a poultice that had been filled with dead flies. When they took it off and showed the patient the flies he naturally thought they had come out of his head—and immediately recovered from his delusion.

2ND DOCTOR: Then there was the man who, after a feverish illness, believed that it would flood the country if he made water. There was no convincing him and he declared himself ready to die to save the people. This gave his doctor an idea. He arranged with the military authorities to send him word of an impending siege and to say that the town moats needed filling and would he please help. The patient was so delighted at being able to save the people and himself into the bargain that he parted with his water and his illness both together.

1ST DOCTOR: I am reminded of the man who imagined his nose

to be ten foot long. He used to go about warning everybody to keep out of the way.

2ND DOCTOR: No doubt, doctor, you have heard of the young man who persisted in thinking that he was dead. He got into a coffin and would neither eat nor drink. His friends tried all manner of tricks, but he only laughed at them, saying that, of course, dead men never ate or drank. However, an experienced doctor succeeded in curing him in the end. This doctor got his servant to feign death. They laid him beside the sick man, and for a time the two lay looking at each other. Then the sick man asked the servant what he had come for, and the servant replied " because he was dead ". After a time they brought the newcomer his supper, and he rose from his coffin, saying to the sick man, " Aren't you going to have yours? " In time the sick man was persuaded to eat and then sleep, get up, dress, and do everything the other man did until, in due course, he was completely cured.

1ST DOCTOR: I have known lots of other cases of delusions. It's just the same with your lordship. Fancy your lordship imagining yourself to be a peasant! But your lordship must try to get the idea out of your mind.

JEPPE: So you really think I've been having ideas?

2ND DOCTOR: Of course! Your lordship has heard of these other cases of delusion.

JEPPE: Then do you mean to say I'm not Jeppe Berg?

1ST DOCTOR: Of course not!

JEPPE: And I'm not married to Nille?

2ND DOCTOR: Not at all! Your lordship is a widower.

JEPPE: Then there's no such thing as Master Eric?

2ND DOCTOR: Master Eric?

JEPPE: Her stick that she wallops me with.

1ST DOCTOR: All imagination!

JEPPE: And it isn't true that she sent me to market to get some soft soap?

2ND DOCTOR: How can it be?

JEPPE: And I didn't spend the money getting drunk at Jacob's?

VALET: Your lordship was out shooting all day yesterday. We were with your lordship.

JEPPE: And you mean to say I'm not a cuckold?

VALET: Your lordship's wife died years ago.

JEPPE: I'm feeling better already! What a nightmare I must have had! Funny how a man can get such queer ideas into his head!

VALET: Would your lordship care to take a walk in the garden while breakfast is being prepared?

1ST DOCTOR: That would do you good.

JEPPE: Oh, all right then. Only hurry up! I'm hungry! And I've a thirst on me like a fish!

ERIC: This way, your lordship.

JEPPE *goes out, followed by* FOOTMEN. *When he is safely out of earshot the* VALET *and the* TWO DOCTORS *enjoy a good laugh before going out at the other door. Almost immediately the* VALET *re-enters with* SECRETARY *and more* FOOTMEN *carrying a table. The* FOOTMEN *draw a curtain to conceal the bed and proceed to lay the table under the* SECRETARY'S *and the* VALET'S *directions. All this takes place to the accompaniment of discreet laughter and by-play. They are all thoroughly enjoying themselves. Presently, when the table has been laid,* JEPPE *re-enters with* ERIC *and the other* FOOTMAN.

JEPPE (*rubbing his hands in anticipation*): Ah, breakfast at last! This looks all right!

VALET: Breakfast is ready, if it pleases your lordship to be seated.

JEPPE *sits down. The others stand round the table and behind his chair. They laugh and exchange signs as he puts his fingers into dishes, belches, wipes his mouth on his sleeve, etc.*

VALET: What wine would it please your lordship to take this morning?

JEPPE: You know, as well as I do, what wine I usually have for breakfast.

VALET: Well, here's the hock your lordship usually prefers. (*He fills his glass.*) It can be changed if it's not to your lordship's taste.

JEPPE (*after taking a gulp at it*): Too sour! Take it away! Some mead might improve it, though. I have a sweet taste. You know I have.

VALET: Here's some canary, if your lordship will taste that. This is sweeter. (*He pours out another glassful.*)

JEPPE (*drinking*): That's the stuff! This tastes all right! Good health, everybody.

Each time he drinks, the FOOTMEN *blow a fanfare of trumpets.*

JEPPE: Come on, there! Another glass of that wine! (*To* SECRETARY.) I say, you, where'd you get that ring?

SECRETARY: It's the one you gave me, your lordship.

JEPPE: I don't remember it! Hand it over! I must have been drunk when I gave you that! People don't give rings like that away when they're in their right senses. I'll have to see what else you've wheedled out of me. It's enough for a servant if he gets his board and lodging. I don't remember giving any of you anything else. Why should I? That ring's worth over ten rix-dollars. No, no, my lads. You keep your places and don't start taking advantage of your master's failings. When I'm drunk I'd give my breeches away. But once I'm sober I want 'em back again. What d'ye think Nille would say? Eh? What did I say? There I go again! Better give me another glass o' that canary-bird. Good health! (*There is a flourish of trumpets as before.*) Now listen to me, you fellows! And don't forget! If I get drunk and give you anything I shall want it back in future. Next morning! Got that? Right! Give a servant more than he can put in his belly and he'll never be satisfied. (*To* SECRETARY.) What wages do I pay you?

SECRETARY: Your lordship has always allowed me 200 rix-dollars a year.

JEPPE: What! 200 rix-dollars! You're damn well not going to get 200 rix-dollars in future! Here I go, sweating and slaving from morning till night and never get——Damn it, there I go again! Another glass o' that wine, there! (*Once again there is a flourish of trumpets as he drinks.*) 200 rix-dollars! You—you bloodsucker! Now listen here, all of you! When I've had my breakfast, I'm going to hang you—every man jack of you! That'll learn you to come squeezing money out o' me!

SECRETARY: Your lordship shall have it all back. None of us ever had any intention of robbing your lordship.

JEPPE: Oh, yes! Your lordship! Your lordship!! Fine words and flattery—they're cheap, aren't they? You'll butter me with " your lordship " till you've wheedled all my money out of me, and that'll be an end of " your lordship ". I know! " Your lordship! " That's what you say! But it isn't what you think, is it? You'll be calling me " you fool " behind my back. You two-faced villains, you! You'd poison a man as soon as look at him! But don't you run away with the idea that Jeppe's a fool! Oh, no!! (*They are all on their knees begging his pardon in mock humility.*) Get up, you dogs! Just wait till I've finished my breakfast! I'll show you! I'm going to string you up on the nearest tree—one after the other. Where's my bailiff?

SECRETARY: In the next room, your lordship.

JEPPE: Fetch him in!

A FOOTMAN *goes out and re-enters immediately with the* BAILIFF, *who wears a coat with silver buttons and a decorated belt as symbol of his rank.*

BAILIFF: Your lordship sent for me?

JEPPE: Yes. Do you know what for?

BAILIFF: No, your lordship.

JEPPE: I'm going to have you hanged.

BAILIFF: Hanged, your lordship? But what have I done, your lordship?

JEPPE: You're the bailiff, aren't you?

BAILIFF: Yes, your lordship.

JEPPE: And you ask me what I'm going to hang you for?

BAILIFF: Yes, your lordship. I've always served your lordship well. I've worked hard, and your lordship has always spoken well of me.

JEPPE: Yes, you've worked hard all right! Collecting silver buttons to put on that coat of yours!! What wages do you get? Eh?

BAILIFF: Fifty rix-dollars a year, your lordship.

JEPPE (*pacing the room*): Fifty rix-dollars, you say. Right! We'll have you hanged straight away!

BAILIFF: You couldn't pay me less, your lordship. I work hard all the year round.

JEPPE: That's why you're going to be hanged. Because I only

pay you fifty rix-dollars a year. And yet you've money for silver buttons, for rings on your fingers, and for a silk purse to show off with. But you only get fifty rix-dollars a year. Don't tell me you've never robbed me! Where else would you get your money from, you dog? Eh? Tell me that?

BAILIFF (*on his knees*): Oh, your lordship, spare me! Spare me for the sake of my wife and children!

JEPPE: Children! How many have you got?

BAILIFF: Seven, your lordship.

JEPPE: Ha! ha! Seven children! Take him away and hang him, Mr. Sekkertary.

SECRETARY: Your lordship, I'm not a hangman.

JEPPE: Oh, so you're not a hangman, eh? That's no reason why you shouldn't become one. You look the sort of fellow that could turn his hand to anything. Take him away, string him up from the nearest tree, and come back here. Then I'll hang you.

BAILIFF: Oh, your lordship, pardon me!

JEPPE *paces up and down, sits down and has another drink, and gets up again.*

JEPPE: Fifty rix-dollars! A wife and seven children. If nobody else'll hang you, I'll have to do it myself. I know you, you bailiffs. I've seen the way you've treated other poor peasants besides me. . . . Oh, there I go again! I mean, I know you and your class. As well as I know the back o' my hand! You skim the cream off everything. All you want is some poor peasant to cross your palm and you go straight away to your master with a " Oh, sir, the poor man is willing and hard-working enough, but he's had a run of bad luck and can't pay his rent. You see, sir, his land's sour, his cattle have had the plague—and so on and so forth." And your master has to make the best of it. No, no, my man, you can't cheat me! I know you! I've had some! Aren't I a peasant myself—Eh, er—I mean—aren't we all Adam's children and peasants in a way.

SECRETARY (*also on his knees*): Oh, your lordship, have pity on him for his poor wife's sake! How could she keep seven children without him?

JEPPE: Why should she keep 'em? Let 'em go hang! Her as well!

SECRETARY: Oh, sir, you wouldn't hang such a pretty woman!

JEPPE: Pretty, eh? Sounds as though you're sweet on her. Go fetch her in.

The BAILIFF *goes out and fetches his* WIFE, *who advances to* JEPPE *and kisses his hand.*

JEPPE (*ogling her*): So you're the bailiff's wife, eh?

WIFE: Yes, your lordship.

JEPPE (*fondling her*): A pretty lass, eh? Come to my room tonight, will you? Eh?

WIFE: As your lordship pleases. I'm in your lordship's service.

JEPPE (*to* BAILIFF): What d'ye say, bailiff?

BAILIFF: Your lordship does me a great honour.

JEPPE (*to* SECRETARY): Hi, you, bring a chair up for the lady! Put it next to mine.

The SECRETARY *does as he is told and she sits down beside* JEPPE, *eating and drinking with him.* JEPPE *fancies he sees the* SECRETARY *making eyes at her, and is immediately jealous.*

JEPPE: You keep your eyes off her, will you?

Whenever he looks at the SECRETARY, *the latter drops his eyes.* JEPPE *puts his arm round the* BAILIFF'S WIFE, *and in a maudlin voice begins to sing a popular love song.*

JEPPE: A dance! A dance! A dance, I say! Let's have a polka!

One of the FOOTMEN *produces a fiddle and starts to play; and* JEPPE *dances round the room with the* BAILIFF'S WIFE. *Three times he lurches and sprawls on the floor but manages to regain his feet. The fourth time he stays on the floor, dead drunk, and almost immediately falls asleep, snoring heavily.*

SECRETARY: Drunk! Dead drunk!! Drunk as a lord!!! (*There is a general burst of laughter.*) Fetch the Baron, one of you. (*Exit* FOOTMAN.) Drunk as a lord! (*Turning* JEPPE *over with his foot.*) So you thought you would hang us all, did you? It's your turn to be hanged now.

Enter BARON, *followed by* FOOTMAN.

BARON (*with a glance at* JEPPE): Well, I see we've won the first round. He's asleep all right.

SECRETARY: He was bent on playing the tyrant with us, my lord.

Said he was going to hang us all as soon as he had finished his breakfast.

BARON: You see the result of too easily gained power. What have I told you? Sudden power, like sudden wealth and too much drink, goes to a man's head.

SECRETARY: It wasn't too soon he fell asleep, my lord. If he'd gone on bullying and badgering us much longer we should have been forced to show our hand.

BARON: And to think that I nearly made the mistake of masquerading as my own secretary for the fun of it! If I'd allowed myself to be bullied and ordered about by him I should have made myself a laughing-stock indeed. I suppose we'd better leave him where he is for a while before you put his peasant's clothes on him again.

ERIC: There's no danger of waking him, my lord. He sleeps like a log. Look, I can roll him over with my foot and he never notices it.

BARON: Very well, then. Take him away, and let's finish the comedy.

They carry JEPPE *out as the* CURTAIN *falls.*

ACT THREE

Scene One

The scene is the same as in Act One. JEPPE, *in his peasant clothes again, is fast asleep on the dung-hill. Presently he wakes and, without looking up, calls out:*

JEPPE: Hi, sekkertary, valet, lackeys! Another glass o' that canary-bird!

Sitting up and gradually becoming conscious, he gazes round him and rubs his eyes. He puts his hand to his head and finds his peasant cap. He rubs his eyes again, turns the hat over in his hands, and looks at his clothes. It is only too clear that he is his old self again, and he gives vent to a loud groan.

JEPPE: Oh!!! I knew it! I knew it! I'm myself again! I knew it was too good to last! How long was Adam in Eden? The same breeches, the same cuckoldy hat, the same—bed! Ugh!! No more canary-bird, no fancy glasses to drink out of, and no lackeys to stand behind my chair! I might have known it! Oh, oh, your lordship, you've come down in the world! Your bed's turned into a muck-heap and your lackeys are only pigs! And you're just a miserable peasant! There was I expecting to wake up and find rings on my fingers, and what's on 'em now? Faugh!! I wish I was back where I was before! I'll go to sleep again and see what happens.

He lies down, and presently is snoring heavily again. NILLE *appears from the cottage.*

NILLE: I wonder what can have happened to him. I hope he hasn't had an accident. More likely to be in some tavern drinking my money up! A fool I was to trust the drunken pig! Hullo, what's this? It's him, the villain! Fast asleep on the muck-heap! Fancy being married to that! I'll make you pay for this, you sot!

She goes into the cottage to get her stick, and then stealing up to JEPPE *she swipes him over the buttocks with it.*

JEPPE: Ow! Ow!! Help! Help!! What's that? Where am I? Who's that? What have I done? Ooh!!

NILLE: I'll teach you who it is, I will!

She lets fly at him again, and then finally pulls him up by the hair.

JEPPE: Don't, Nille! Nille, love, don't hit me any more! You'll kill me! You've no idea where I've been!

NILLE: No, you drunken villain; that's just what I'd like to know! Where's that soft soap I sent you to get? Eh?

JEPPE: I haven't got any, Nille. I never got there.

NILLE: And why didn't you get there? That's what I want to know! Out with it! Where have you been?

JEPPE: Nille, I think I've been in Heaven.

NILLE (*as she belabours him with the stick again*): Heaven! Heaven, did you say? I'll Heaven you!! I'll teach you to come making jokes at my expense!!

JEPPE: Ow! Ow!! Ow!!! It's as true as I'm standing here, Nille!

NILLE: What's true?

JEPPE: That I've been in Heaven.

NILLE: You scoundrel, you! I'll give you Heaven!

JEPPE: Oh, Nille, dear, don't hit me!

NILLE: Then tell me where you've been, you wretch! Or I'll thrash you within an inch of your life!

JEPPE: Promise not to hit me, then, Nille.

NILLE: Out with it!

JEPPE: Promise not to hit me, Nille!

NILLE: I'll promise nothing!

JEPPE: As true as I'm standing here, Nille, I think I've been in Heaven. And I've seen things that'd surprise you. As sure as my name's Jeppe.

NILLE, *giving him up as hopeless, drags him to the cottage, and, opening the door, pushes him in.*

NILLE: There, you drunken pig! Stop there and sleep it off! And then we'll see about it! Heaven! Him!! Hell's more fit for the likes of him!!! Cock and bull stories!!! He'll get no more drink with money of mine! And if he gets anything to eat today or tomorrow he can think himself lucky. That'll teach him a lesson.

Enter TWO MEMBERS OF THE WATCH, *who make for the cottage.*

NILLE: Well, what do *you* want?

1ST MAN: Is this where Jeppe Berg lives?

NILLE: Yes, it is. What for?

1ST MAN: Are you his wife?

NILLE: Yes, God help me!

1ST MAN: We want a word with him.

NILLE: He's drunk.

1ST MAN: Never mind about that. Fetch him out. And no nonsense, or it'll be the worse for the two of you.

NILLE *goes into the cottage and pushes* JEPPE *out, so that he collides with one of the men and bowls him over.*

JEPPE: There's a wife for you! You see what I have to put up with!

1ST MAN: You deserve all you get, you villain!

JEPPE: What have I done now?

1ST MAN: You'll find out when you get before the Magistrate. You're arrested. You'd better come quietly.

They bustle him off.

NILLE: Serve him right! Good riddance to bad rubbish!

CURTAIN

ACT THREE

Scene Two

A court-room. COURT OFFICIALS, *with* COUNSEL FOR THE PROSECUTION AND DEFENCE, *rise as the* MAGISTRATE *enters followed by his* CLERK. *The* MAGISTRATE *takes his seat and the Court settles down again. There is a general air of mock solemnity, and in fact this is only a mock trial. The* MAGISTRATE *is the* BARON *and the various officials are members of his household.*

MAGISTRATE: Call the prisoner.

The cry is taken up by ushers and JEPPE *is brought in, his hands bound behind his back.*

MAGISTRATE: Proceed with the case.

PROSECUTOR: This is the man, your worship. Jeppe Berg. I charge him with breaking into the Manor and impersonating the Baron, and with bullying and ill-treating the Baron's servants. Acting on the Baron's behalf, I demand that the prisoner be severely punished in order to teach him a lesson.

MAGISTRATE: Is the charge true, my man? What have you to say for yourself? Speak up!

JEPPE: What can I say? I can only say that I've done nothing to deserve this. I own up to spending the wife's money on drink. And I own up to being at the Baron's. But how I got there and how I got away again, I haven't the least idea.

PROSECUTOR: That's enough! Your worship has heard the prisoner's confession from his own lips. He confesses to having been drunk and to committing the offence with which he is charged. What more need be said, your worship? I submit that drunkenness is no excuse. If it were, every criminal would plead drunkenness. It is a clear case, your worship, and there is no need to waste the court's time any further.

MAGISTRATE: Counsel for the Defence, what have you to say?

DEFENCE COUNSEL: Your worship, I submit that the charge is far-fetched. In fact it is preposterous. How could a simple peasant gain entry to the Manor and assume the Baron's identity, while clearly unable to assume the Baron's face or figure? I submit that the whole story is an invention by this man's enemies. I demand that he be unconditionally discharged.

JEPPE (*almost in tears*): God bless your soul, good sir! Here, have a chew o' my tobacco. It's all I have to give you, but it's a good 'bacca.

DEFENCE COUNSEL: No, keep your tobacco, Jeppe. I'm not doing this for payment.

JEPPE: Beg pardon, sir, I'm sure! I never thought lawyers were so decent!

PROSECUTOR: My colleague's submissions are based on conjecture. We are not concerned with probability, but with fact. The prisoner has confessed.

DEFENCE COUNSEL: Confessions under duress are not valid evidence, your worship. I submit that the prisoner be given an opportunity to consider what he is saying. Now, Jeppe, think what you are saying. Do you confess to the charge that has been brought against you?

JEPPE: No, what I said before was all lies. I'll take my oath on it. It's three days since I set foot outside my own door.

PROSECUTOR: Your worship, I submit that it is out of order for a prisoner to make new testimony in court after he has confessed to the offence he has been charged with.

DEFENCE COUNSEL: I submit that it is in order.

PROSECUTOR: I submit that it is not.

DEFENCE COUNSEL: Certainly it is, in a case of this nature.

PROSECUTOR: Your worship, the man has already confessed to the crime.

JEPPE (*rubbing his hands*): Go on! Have a go at one another! Then I can have a go at the Magistrate. I'll knock some sense into his head, if I get a chance.

DEFENCE COUNSEL: But, your worship, what crime has the prisoner confessed to? He admits to being on the premises, but that is all, your worship. Did he commit theft, or violence?

PROSECUTOR: Irrelevant! There was intent to commit a crime. If a man is seized when about to steal, he is as guilty as if he had been caught in the very act.

JEPPE: Your worship, I'd gladly hang if this fellow could hang with me.

DEFENCE COUNSEL: Hold your tongue, Jeppe. You're only spoiling your own case.

JEPPE: Then why don't you answer him?

DEFENCE COUNSEL: But what proof is there of any intention even to commit a crime?

PROSECUTOR: *Quicunque in ædes alienas noctu irrumpit, tanquem fur aut nocturnus grassator, existimandus est ; atqui reus hic ita, ergo . . .*

DEFENCE COUNSEL: *Nego majorem, quod scilicet irruperit.*

PROSECUTOR: *Res manifesta est, tot legitimis testibus exstantibus, ac confitente reo.*

DEFENCE COUNSEL: *Quicunque vi vel metu coactum fuerit cofiteri . . .*

PROSECUTOR: Then where is this *vis*! Where is this *metus*? It's all red tape.

DEFENCE COUNSEL: Red tape! You dare to accuse me of red tape?

PROSECUTOR: This is the limit!

They fly at each other's throat and JEPPE *seizes the opportunity to get behind the* PROSECUTING COUNSEL *and tear his wig off.*

MAGISTRATE: Silence in court! Order! Order there! Be seated, gentlemen! I have heard sufficient. This is my judgment. (*As he takes up a scroll.*) Whereas Jeppe Berg, of this place, having confessed to gaining illegal access to the Baron's Manor, putting on his clothes, and ill-treating his servants, be it known that he is hereby sentenced to death by poisoning, his dead body to be hung from the gibbet.

JEPPE: Oh, oh, your worship, have mercy on me! I never meant to do any harm!

MAGISTRATE: No mercy is possible. Let the sentence be carried out in my presence.

JEPPE: Please, your worship, can I have a drop o' gin first, before I drink the poison? I'll die like a man then.

MAGISTRATE: Your wish is granted, Bring the prisoner his gin.

A bottle and a glass are brought, and JEPPE *drinks three glassfuls.*

JEPPE (*on his knees*): Mercy, your worship!

MAGISTRATE: No, Jeppe, it's too late.

JEPPE: It's never too late, your worship. Change the verdict and say you made a mistake. We all make mistakes sometimes.

MAGISTRATE: No. In a few seconds you'll feel that it is too late. You see, Jeppe, you drank the poison with the gin.

JEPPE: Oh, oh, oh!! I'm going to die!! Farewell, Nille! You cat, you don't deserve this! Farewell, my children! Farewell, my piebald nag! Farewell, Cæsar, my faithful friend and watch-dog! Farewell, all my cows and pigs! Farewell! Oh, I'm going to die! I feel so weak and heavy! Worse than when I was drunk! Oh, I'm dying!

And he falls to the floor unconscious.

MAGISTRATE: Right! The drug has taken effect. Now he'll sleep like a log. Take him and hang him up near his own cottage. But see you don't hurt him. Tie the rope under his armpits. We'll see what happens when he wakes up and finds himself on the gibbet.

They carry him out.

CURTAIN

Act Three

Scene Three

The scene is the same as in Act One. Jeppe *is hanging by his arms from a gibbet that has been set up somewhere in the centre of the stage.* Nille *is kneeling in front of it, weeping. Hidden from view of both, but visible to the audience, are the* Magistrate *and* Court Officials, *alias the* Baron *and his* Attendants.

Nille: Oh, oh! To think that it should come to this! That he should end his days on a gibbet! Jeppe, Jeppe, forgive me for all I did to you! I never really meant it! If I could only have saved him. I'd have done anything! But now it's—it's too late! Too late!!

She breaks down in tears. Meanwhile Jeppe *has come round and has realized where he is and what is going on.*

Jeppe: Don't take it too hard, Nille, dear! You haven't been such a bad wife! We all have to come to it. Go and look after the home and our children. You'll be all right. And, Nille, alter my red coat. It'll come in for Christopher. The rest will make a hat for Martha. See that my piebald mare gets treated properly. If I wasn't so dead there'd be a lot more to say to you. Now don't you worry, Nille. Don't take things too much to heart.

Nille: Eh? What's that? Was that him talking?

Jeppe: Don't be scared, Nille. I'm not going to hurt you.

Nille: Jeppe, I thought you were dead! How can you talk when you're dead?

Jeppe: How do I know? Listen, Nille, my love; go and get me a drop o' gin. I've got the biggest thirst I've ever had in my life! I mean, bigger than I ever had in my life!

Nille: Faugh, you beast, you sot, you drunken swine, you! Didn't you get enough when you were alive? Are you going to go on guzzling gin now you're dead? You—you worthless scoundrel, you!!

JEPPE: Hold your tongue, you hag! And go and get that gin when I tell you!

NILLE: And supposing I refuse, you hound?

JEPPE: You'll wish you hadn't. Because I'll—I'll haunt you every night of your life! Just you see if I don't! I'll show you! I'm not scared o' your Master Eric now, you know! Oh, no! I'm past that!! And a good job, and all!!

NILLE *is already in the cottage, and in a moment is back with Master Eric, with which she proceeds to belabour* JEPPE.

NILLE: So you're not afraid of Master Eric, eh? We'll soon see! Take that! And that!! And that!!!

JEPPE: Ow, ow, ow!!! Stop it, Nille! Stop it!! You're killing me!!! Ow, ow—!

NILLE: That'll teach you! I'll give you gin!!

The MAGISTRATE *comes forward from his place of concealment.*

MAGISTRATE: Now, now, my good woman, that will do! You mustn't go on striking your husband. For your sake, I'm going to pardon him and sentence him to life again. And I hope this will be a lesson to you both.

NILLE: Oh, no, your worship! Let him hang! It's all he's good for!

MAGISTRATE: Fie on you, woman! Off you go, or I'll have you hung up beside him. You should be ashamed of yourself.

THE MAGISTRATE'S ATTENDANTS *come forward.* NILLE *is scared now and runs away.*

MAGISTRATE: Take him down. (*They do so.*)

JEPPE: Oh, your worship, is it true I'm alive again?

MAGISTRATE: Yes, Jeppe.

JEPPE: Are you sure it's me, your worship? And not my ghost?

MAGISTRATE: No, it's not your ghost. You're alive all right.

JEPPE: How can I be alive when I was dead?

MAGISTRATE: Don't you see that you have been sentenced back to life again? A court can always reverse its decisions. Can't you see that?

JEPPE: No, I'm hanged if I see it! I mean—No, I don't mean, I mean—I mean I think I'm haunted!

MAGISTRATE: You foolish man! It's simple enough to

understand. Supposing somebody gives you something. They can always take it back, can't they?

JEPPE: I suppose they can.

MAGISTRATE: And supposing they take it away. They can always give it back to you, can't they?

JEPPE: Er—I suppose they—Eh? Suppose you let me hang you, your worship! And then sentence you to life again!

MAGISTRATE: That's impossible. You are not a magistrate.

JEPPE: No. But—but—do you really mean to say I'm alive again?

MAGISTRATE: Of course not.

JEPPE: And I'm not haunted?

MAGISTRATE: No, no.

JEPPE: You're sure I'm not a ghost?

MAGISTRATE: Perfectly sure.

JEPPE: I'm Jeppe Berg. The same as I used to be?

MAGISTRATE: Why, yes.

JEPPE: I'm alive? Will you swear it?

MAGISTRATE: Yes, I swear you are alive.

JEPPE: You'll take your oath on it?

MAGISTRATE: Now believe what I say and be grateful to me for letting you off.

JEPPE: I'd have been grateful if you hadn't hung me up in the first place.

MAGISTRATE: Now be content, Jeppe. And next time your wife beats you, you come and complain to me or the Baron about it. We'll soon deal with her. Here! This is for yourself. Cheer up! Don't forget to drink my health, but don't overdo the gin another time. If I catch you drunk again you'll not get off so lightly.

JEPPE *kisses the* MAGISTRATE'S *hand.*

JEPPE: Thank you, your worship. I'ts nice to be alive.

The MAGISTRATE *goes off with his suite.* JEPPE *stands bewildered for a while, then looks at the coin in his hand, spits on it, and rubs it on his sleeve.*

JEPPE: Hurray! I'm alive!! Alive!!! Phew, what a life! A peasant! Drunk! A baron! Drunk! A peasant again! Then hanged! Then brought to life again! I don't know whether

I'm awake or dreaming! But there's one thing I do know! (*He strides over to the inn door, and hammers on it.*) Hi, Jacob! Open the door there, will you?

JACOB (*at the door*): Oh, it's you, is it? What's brought you now?

JEPPE: A thirst, Jacob! Give us a glass o' gin, will you?

CURTAIN

END OF PLAY

THE ARABIAN POWDER

(*Det arabiske Pulver*)

A Comedy in One Act

1724

CHARACTERS

POLIDOR, a dabbler in alchemy
LEONORA, his wife
HENRIK } their servants
PERNILLA }
FOX, a rogue
ANDREAS, his crony
BENJAMIN, a go-between
LEANDER, a gentleman
LEANDER'S WIFE
A POET
A GENTLEMAN
LANDLORD of the " Pheasant "
Ladies and Gentlemen

SCENE: A street outside Polidor's house in a Danish provincial town

TIME: About 1720

THE ARABIAN POWDER

The scene is a street outside POLIDOR'S *house in a Danish provincial town, about* 1720.

Enter FOX, *looking interestedly around him ; he is a stranger in the town and has just arrived.*

FOX: H'm, a bigger place than I thought. Nice houses in it, too. Should be some money about, by the look of it. (ANDREAS *enters from the other side, and* FOX *at once recognizes an old crony.*) Why, if it isn't my old friend Andreas! Hullo there, Andreas, my lad! Is it you? Or only your ghost!

ANDREAS (*who is wearing a black fur cap pulled well down over his head and a black eye-shield*): Fox! Well, I never! Fancy meeting you here! It's ages since I clapped eyes on you! How are you, Foxey, old man? Glad to see you! (*And they shake hands and clap one another on the shoulder with every sign of pleasure at reunion.*)

FOX: Well, well! You could 'ave knocked me down with a feather! Why, I thought they'd strung you up years ago. But you're no fool, Andreas. You know your job, you do. Pinching's easy, I always say. Any fool of a beginner can pinch. But to pinch and get away with it—now, that's what I call knowing your job!

ANDREAS: It's decent of you to say so, Foxey, old man. Coming from you, that's real praise. You know, I've a lot to thank the old folks for. If ever a man had a proper upbringing, it was me; and it's seen me through every time. All but once. I was nabbed once. Though it might have been worse when you come to think of it—only lost my ears.

FOX: Pooh! What's a pair of lugs to an able-bodied fellow like you? So that's what you're wearing that cap for, is it?

ANDREAS: That's it, Foxey. And that's why I never raise my cap any more. Just put my hand up to it; like an officer taking the salute. (*He suits the action to the word.*) They think I'm swelled-headed. But that's just where they're mistaken;

I'm not so swelled-headed as I used to be! But what about you, Foxey? How's the world been using you?

Fox: Me? Oh, can't grumble. I manage to rub along; get on all right with most people. All but these damned law officers! Never could mind their own business, they couldn't! It isn't above a fortnight since one of 'em came poking his nose into my affairs—and me into a poky little place without as much as a "by your leave"! I gave 'em the slip, though! Law!! There's not much to be had out of the law by such as us, Andreas.

Andreas: You're right, there Fox! Never leave a fellow alone, do they? Jealous, that's what they are!

Fox: Jealous!! No sooner see a chap making an honest penny than they're out to get it.

Andreas: There's no peace for the virtuous!

Fox: Worst of the lot are the ones in your own town. It's a fact. I've sworn never to go near mine again.

Andreas: And what's brought you to this place, Fox? Can't be much in your line here.

Fox: Oh, I don't know. I can turn my hand to anything. Now, you should have seen me at Augsburg.

Andreas: Augsburg! That's in Germany, isn't it?

Fox: Right! And what do you think I was doing there?

Andreas: Ask me another!

Fox: Doctoring!

Andreas: What, horse-doctoring?

Fox: No, proper doctoring. I had a nice little practice, too. I'd have had it yet but for the same old trouble. Jealousy again! The doctors, this time. If they didn't call in the law officers and threaten to have me hanged! The patients were all right; they never complained.

Andreas: They wouldn't have a chance! Didn't live long enough, eh?

Fox: And what if they didn't? They got rid of their ailments, didn't they? The way those doctor fellows used to torment their patients, year in and year out—it was a disgrace! Me—why, I never bothered any of 'em more than three days. You know, lots of well-to-do folk in Augsburg owe all they've got to me. Where'd they be if I hadn't cured their parents for 'em—Waiting for their fortunes yet! Doctors! The jealous, backbiting thieves! As for the law officers, they'd sentence you as soon as look at you.

ANDREAS: Right again, Foxey, old man! And once let 'em hang you, and you can appeal till your black and blue in the face for all the good it'll do you. So you hopped it, eh?

FOX: Moved on to Nuremberg. And what d'you think I took up there? Fortune-telling! Made quite a name, I did, too. But then a fellow can't always be on form. And when I made one or two mistakes, blow me, if they didn't get jealous again! But that's where fortune-telling comes in, my boy. D'you know, I did what many a fortune-teller never could—told my own fortune! "Stop here any longer, Foxey," I said, "and it'll be a bad look-out for you!"

ANDREAS: Call that fortune-telling? I could have told you the same myself, and I'm no fortune-teller.

FOX: Next place I stopped at was Frankfurt. I was a fencing-master there. No end of pupils and all paying in advance. But then, bless me if my conscience didn't start to prick me! Now is it right, I said to myself, to teach these nice young fellows to play about with swords? They might hurt themselves! And rather than that anything like that should happen I—er—I gathered up my belongings—and I gently stole away.

ANDREAS: Without stopping to give 'em their money back?

FOX: Eh? No. Oh, no! I was in a hurry and couldn't find 'em. Besides, I had my travelling expenses, hadn't I? But so's they'd know I was coming back I raised a loan with the landlord. Well now, next place I stopped at was Strasbourg. Went into local politics there.

ANDREAS: And made a good thing out of it, I dare say.

FOX: Oh, not so bad; not so bad. They started offering me jobs just to keep my mouth shut! But that was no good for me—not without a year's salary in advance.

ANDREAS: Did you get it?

FOX: I got it all right. But then I said to myself, "Foxey, my boy," I said, "you're not cut out for this." So I resigned. No fuss, mind you! Oh, no; just walked out quietly without saying a word. Next stop, Cologne. Next job—astronomy.

Then on to London—and alchemy. Last place I stopped at was Antwerp. I started a religious revival there. Money! It rolled in. Collections, you know.

ANDREAS: What made you give that up?

FOX: Jealousy again! Plain professional jealousy!! There was I holding forth in the street one day, when who should walk up but Smit! You know Smit! What d'you think he did? Laughed in my face! Had the cheek to tell my audience I was the biggest rogue and liar on God's earth. Of course, they didn't believe him. Not they! They'd have mobbed him, but for me. Still, I thought it was time to be moving.

ANDREAS: So you moved on to here! And what's the next scheme?

FOX: Couldn't say. But I'll let you into my scheme for finding out. Count my buttons! Last button decides. (*Counts.*) Doctor, fortune-teller, fencing-master, confidence man, politician, alchemist, preacher. No, that won't do. Must have a change. Try again. (*Counts a second time and comes to an end at alchemist.*) Alchemist. Right; alchemist it is, then! I'm going to make gold, I am. And you're going to help me, Andreas.

ANDREAS: Me? How?

FOX: You just listen to me, my lad, and I'll tell you. Now guess what's in this bag. (*He takes a small bag from his pocket.*) Gold! Powdered gold!! What you might call a sprat to catch a mackerel, Andreas. Now I'll tell you where you come in. You open a stall in the market, and among your wares you offer this powder for sale. But you don't sell it unless you're asked for Arabian powder. Got that! *Arabian powder.* Right! That's all you need bother *your* head about. Leave the rest to me. And it won't be long before that powder's turning itself into gold coins—and a quarter of the winnings are yours, Andreas. So the sooner you get started, the better. Here's the powder. How long do you need to get ready?

ANDREAS: Foxey, you're a marvel! Give me half-an-hour.

FOX: Right! Now remember—Arabian powder. And rely on your uncle. (ANDREAS *hurries off.*) Good old Andreas! Stroke o' luck, meeting him.

BENJAMIN (*who has entered from the other side*): Good morning, sir. Excuse me, sir. You have something to sell, sir?

FOX: Eh? No, not today, old man. I've only just come. Call again tomorrow. Just let me get to work first, and there may be some gold. But—look here, though—you'd better keep that to yourself. I don't want all the town to know.

BENJAMIN: What you say? You make gold?

FOX: A bit. Just enough to keep me going. Never more than a month's supply at a time——

BENJAMIN: Gold! I say, sir, if you want to do business, I know a man——

FOX: If he wants to know how to do it the charge is 4,000 rix-dollars. What's the name of this man of yours?

BENJAMIN: Polidor, sir. This is his house.

FOX: You don't say!

BENJAMIN: He'll give you 4,000 rix-dollars. Why, he's been trying to make gold for years, he has; and never had any luck yet.

FOX: What sort of man is he, this Polidor?

BENJAMIN: A nice gentleman, sir. Oh, a very nice gentleman, sir. A man that has studied a lot.

FOX: Studied! It's a waste of time. Anybody can make gold. All it wants is patience—that and one or two little secrets of my own.

BENJAMIN: The trouble is, sir, he's been cheated so many times I'm afraid he won't believe you, sir.

FOX: The gentleman does right to be careful. There's a lot of tricksters about these days. But don't you worry. He needn't believe anything—not till I've delivered the goods. I'm not offering a pig in a poke, I'm not.

BENJAMIN: Do you extract your gold from other metals, sir?

FOX: No, not me. It isn't worth the bother. I can make the stuff out of anything. Well, I must be getting back to my lodgings. Can't stay here talking all day.

BENJAMIN: Where—where are your lodgings, sir?

FOX: At "The Pheasant". Just round the corner. You call there tomorrow, if you want to see some gold.

BENJAMIN: Good, good! I'll be there tomorrow, sir. (*And* FOX, *having set his bait, goes off.*) Gold! Says he can make it!! The fellow seemed to have an honest face. But I'll believe it when I see it. Better hurry up and tell Master Polidor, though. There'll be some nice commission on this. (*He knocks at the front door, and it is opened by* HENRIK.)

HENRIK: Who do you want, Benjamin?

BENJAMIN: Master Polidor, Henrik, if he's in.

HENRIK: Sorry, Benjy, but you can't see him. He's having one of his fits.

BENJAMIN: His what?

HENRIK: Fits. What did I say?

BENJAMIN: Fits? How long's he been having these?

HENRIK: Off and on these last ten years.

BENJAMIN: Oh, get away, Henrik! I've known him for years and I've never heard of them.

HENRIK: All right, then. I say he's having a fit. Yes, a fit. When a man spends a hot summer's day puffing and sweating over a red-hot furnace, what else would you call it but a fit?—A mad fit!

BENJAMIN (*laughing*): Oh, now I understand. So he's in his laboratory, is he?

HENRIK: Laboratory or lavatory, it's all the same to me. The hours he spends in there! Looking for gold! Gold!! And how much has he found? Not that much!! Not enough to buy a noose to hang himself with. Because, mind you, that's what it'll come to, the way he goes wasting all his time and money on it. And when he's in there he hasn't a word for the cat. He'll see nobody and he'll speak to nobody. You can take it from me—so you needn't wait.

BENJAMIN: He'll see me, all right, Henrik. You tell him Benjamin—er—knows a man—a man who can make gold. Tell him that, Henrik. And tell him he'll show him how to do it without payment till he's seen the result.

HENRIK: Gold, did you say? He'll see you about that, all right. You tell him the house is on fire; tell him somebody's assaulting his wife; tell him the burglars are in the house. Will he come? Not he? Not when he's in there. And catch me trying to get him to! But gold! He'll be there in a jiffy!!

BENJAMIN: You go straight in then, Henrik, and tell him. Don't waste any more time. The man may not be here tomorrow.

HENRIK: I'll call him. I daren't go in. (*Calls round the side of the house.*) Master! Master! Master Polidor!

POLIDOR (*inside*): Be quiet, you dog! Don't you know I'm working?

HENRIK: Master, I've something important to tell you.

POLIDOR: I've something that'll warm your backside! Go away and leave me in peace!

HENRIK (*to* BENJAMIN): What did I tell you! But just listen now. (*To* POLIDOR.) Master, there's a man who knows how to make gold. He'll show you how to do it.

POLIDOR: Eh? What's that? What d'you say? Ask him to wait. I'll be there in a minute.

HENRIK: Didn't I tell you? I knew that'd fetch him.

POLIDOR *appears from the side of the house—a fantastic sight. He is wearing a dazzlingly coloured and patterned dressing-gown, protected by a leather apron in front. A big, wide-brimmed hat is pulled forward over his eyes. In one hand he holds a pair of huge bellows and in the other a pair of tongs of corresponding size. He is black in the face.*

POLIDOR: Where is he? Where's this man who says he can make gold?

BENJAMIN: I've just been talking to him, sir. He's staying at "The Pheasant".

POLIDOR: Er—will he tell anybody how to do it? What did he say, Benjamin?

BENJAMIN: He said he would, sir. But he wants a lot for it.

POLIDOR: How much?

BENJAMIN: 4,000 rix-dollars.

POLIDOR: How much, do you say?

BENJAMIN: 4,000 rix-dollars. That's what he said, sir.

POLIDOR: 4,000 rix-dollars! Why, it's a small fortune.

HENRIK: All depends on the way you look at it, master. What's 4,000 rix-dollars if you can make ten times that much in pure gold?

POLIDOR: What do you say, Henrik, my boy? Would you give him that for it?

HENRIK: You please yourself, master. You can only lose it once, supposing it goes the same way as the rest.

POLIDOR: Er—look ye here, Benjamin. Will you guarantee this man? See he doesn't cheat me, will you?

BENJAMIN: Me? Not me, sir! Why, I've only seen the man once. Let him guarantee himself! But he said he didn't want any money—not till you'd seen the results.

POLIDOR: H'm! Seems fair and reasonable. Go and fetch him, Benjamin. will you? But—I say, look here, though. Pretend you're bringing him yourself. Don't let him think I'm dying to see him, whatever you do.

BENJAMIN: Trust me, sir. I'll go and find him.

POLIDOR: Good, Benjamin. That's the way. I'll see you all right for this.

As BENJAMIN *goes off*, LEONORA *enters from the opposite side, followed by* PERNILLA.

LEONORA: Well really, of all the sights! A nice filthy mess you're in!

POLIDOR: Work, Leonora, my love. What can you expect?

PERNILLA: You may well say "What can you expect?" A precious lot *I* expect to come out of this business, all the years you've been at it!

POLIDOR: Now you keep a civil tongue in your head, Pernilla; and don't go speaking disrespectfully about the noble art of alchemy.

PERNILLA: You do right to call it noble. Only noble people with more money than they know what to do with can afford it. A fat lot of good it'll do you, or any of us!

POLIDOR: Now, now!

PERNILLA: It'll be the road to ruin for the lot of us.

POLIDOR: Now, look here, wife! You shouldn't keep such impudent servants.

LEONORA: My dear, Pernilla's right, as anybody with any sense can see. What have you got out of it, anyway?

POLIDOR: It'll all come at once when it does come.

PERNILLA: It'll all come at once, sure enough! You'll steam, boil, cook, and roast, and one fine day you'll set the house on fire. And then where shall we be? On the streets.

LEONORA: My dear, you've been at it for ten years, now. Another ten, and you'll have to turn to something more useful.

PERNILLA: Selling matches!

POLIDOR: You—you impudent baggage, you! Get in to your spinning wheel! D'ye hear? And you, wife, go in to your embroidery and leave me in peace.

PERNILLA: My mistress will be very glad to go in to her embroidery when you give her some of that gold you've made. Gold embroidery! Won't it look nice?

POLIDOR: The devil take the hussy! I've a good mind to——! All right, then. You just wait and see. You'll be laughing on the other side of your faces when I start making gold.

PERNILLA: When!

POLIDOR: I'll let you into a secret. I've found somebody who's going to show me how to do it.

PERNILLA: Another rogue and cheat!

POLIDOR: Who says he's a rogue and cheat?

PERNILLA: He's an anti-Christ, isn't he? Isn't that what you call a man who makes gold?

POLIDOR: You mean alchemist. But why should he be a rogue and cheat?

PERNILLA: Because he's an—an al-alchemist.

POLIDOR: Hold your tongue, will you? You'll be calling me a cheat soon.

PERNILLA: Well, aren't you?

POLIDOR: What!!

PERNILLA: What else are you? You cheat yourself; your wife; your children. I'll speak my mind, and I don't care what you do. And you can take this from me: it'd do you more good than looking for gold if you was to get somebody to wash the soot and grime off your face. (*And with this final fling she trips off into the house.*)

POLIDOR: You—you—you—! Wife, I won't have that girl in my house an hour longer! I've told you!

LEONORA: Come now, my dear; you musn't take her too seriously. She's a good girl and there was no offence meant.

POLIDOR: And you go inside with her. I've had enough of the pair of you!

LEONORA: Very well, then. As you please. (*She goes in.*)

POLIDOR: No offence meant!

HENRIK: I say, master, here's Benjamin, bringing the gold-maker. And if you ask me, master, he ought to be ashamed of himself—dressing so shabbily when he can make enough gold to buy himself as many new clothes as he likes!

POLIDOR: Which just shows, Henrik, that you don't know us alchemists. We don't believe in outward show. Here, take the bellows and tongs and get me my wig. (HENRIK *runs in and fetches a wig, which he puts on his master's head. Enter* BENJAMIN, *followed by* FOX.)

BENJAMIN: Here's the man, sir. I had a job to persuade him to come. You'd better talk to him yourself, sir.

POLIDOR (*to* FOX): Your servant, sir. I'm very glad to be able to welcome a professional colleague. When did you get here, sir?

FOX: What business is it of yours?

HENRIK (*to* POLIDOR): He's quick-tempered, isn't he?

POLIDOR: Er—the artistic temperament, Henrik, my boy. (*To* FOX.) Can I be of any service to you, sir, during your stay in our town?

FOX: The greatest service you can do me is to stop the ceremony. Service! What sort of service?

POLIDOR: Surely a gentleman can always be of service to another. You're a stranger in this town. I thought I might be able to give you introductions to a few useful people.

FOX: Introductions! I've travelled all over the world, and I've never needed any. Useful people! I've never met any. Only one, but you wouldn't know him—I mean my good friend and master, Elbofagomar-Fagius. He's an Arabian. Ah, now there's a man for you! Kind! Why, he's kinder to dumb animals than most men to their wives. I remember the day his cat was asleep on his sleeve when the gong sounded for prayers. What do you think he did? You'd hardly believe it! So as not to wake the cat, he cut the piece out of his sleeve that it was sitting on!! What do you say to that for kindness?

POLIDOR: Yes, that was kind. I'm afraid we've no such people in this country. Are you from Arabia, sir?

FOX: Now there you go again! No, I'm from the moon. What is it you're fishing for?

POLIDOR: One has to open a conversation somehow.

FOX: I've no use for all these ceremonies. If you've something to say, say it, sir. My time's precious.

POLIDOR: I've—er—well, I've heard of your great skill.

FOX: I dare say.

POLIDOR: And having studied the science of alchemy—for a good many years now—I'm—er—glad to have an opportunity of—of exchanging ideas with you.

FOX: Where have you studied?

POLIDOR: I've read the best authors.

FOX: The best authors are the best fools. They don't understand their own writings. I wasted ten years on studies—and how much wiser d'you think I was when I'd finished? Not much! But the great Elbofagomar-Fagius, now! Ah, now there's a man! Why, in one hour he taught me more than I'd learnt in years of book-reading.

POLIDOR: Would you feel disposed to teach me, sir? For—for a consideration, I mean!

FOX: For six years after I left my master, I refused to teach anybody. In fact, those were his orders, Tell nobody, he said!

POLIDOR: But surely—er—after all this time——

FOX: Well, as a matter of fact, I asked for a special favour not long ago, and I've just got his reply. What do you think he says? (*Takes out a letter.*) Here's his letter; dated the 23rd of the month of Gorael, 603 years from Hegira. Look what he says. (*Reads.*) " Allabricamo Triel Siki, Elmacino Eben Alfantara Masaki Gombada ".

POLIDOR: Eh! What's all that? I don't understand Arabic.

FOX: And he goes on: " Mihynki Carassa Almanzera Tarif Elbrunadora Alcantara ".

POLIDOR: What's he mean by Alcantara? Isn't that a town in Spain?

FOX: Eh? Alcantara; oh, that's a sum of money—4,000 rix-dollars! That's what he allows me to charge for teaching his art—as a special favour.

POLIDOR: You—you could charge less if you wanted to, I suppose?

FOX: Less? No, never. Listen to what he says: " Aitzeda Cranganor Monopotapa Lacandaro Mihopi Madagascar Rencolavet ".

POLIDOR: I tell you I don't understand! But does he say you can't charge less than 4,000 rix-dollars?

FOX: Yes. Didn't you hear? " Mihopi Madagascar Rencolavet."

POLIDOR: Not even if you wanted to? Out of generosity, or for a friend?

FOX: No. And he gives a very good reason. Look! " Bramini Muhamed Nadir Elaocombra Caffares Canunor Elcanen." So if you want to learn the art, it'll cost you 4,000 rix-dollars.

POLIDOR: 4,000 rix-dollars! It's a lot of money! But—look here, sir. Tell me this! What do you want the money for if you can make it?

FOX: I have my master's written orders not to give away his secret for nothing. Besides, see what he says in his letter: " Boamirci Muhamed Nadir ". As for that, sir, I might ask the same question. What's 4,000 rix-dollars to you when all you have to do is to make the money? And plenty more?

POLIDOR: It's quite right what you say, sir. But there's just one thing that worries me. It's——

FOX: Ah, now don't tell me. I think I can guess. You've been swindled so many times before, why trust me?

HENRIK: Well, sir, my master didn't want to be so—so rude. But it's true; he's been taken in a few times, he has.

FOX: It's a fair question, sir, and I can understand your caution. But I don't expect you to trust me, and I'm not asking for any money—not in advance. You can pay me when I've shown you how to do it.

POLIDOR: Right! Then I have an idea. Suppose I give the money to Benjamin here to hold? Then if the results are satisfactory he can hand it over to you. What d'you say to that?

FOX: Agreed, sir! Nothing could be fairer! That's settled, then! Now, I'd like to have a look at your laboratory. We must make sure that you have the proper equipment.

POLIDOR: This way, then, please. (*They go in at the side door*, BENJAMIN *following.*)

HENRIK: I wonder how it'll all turn out! I only hope the master's not going to lose some more of his money! And yet it's in safe keeping till he's seen a fair trial. It's beyond me. Hullo, here's the mistress, and Pernilla.

LEONORA *and* PERNILLA *enter from the front door.*

LEONORA: Henrik, where's your master?

HENRIK: Gone into the workshop. And shall I let you into the news? When he comes out he'll be rolling in money!—Or else we shall all be starving! He's made a bargain with the new gold-maker, and he's bound to be either the one or the other. I'm keeping my fingers crossed!

PERNILLA: You don't mean to say the master's given the fellow money?

HENRIK: The master's giving Benjamin 4,000 rix-dollars to pay the fellow when he's proved he can do what he says he can.

LEONORA: It makes me shudder to think of it! There's some trickery in this, I'll be bound!

HENRIK: Well, I will say the master was very careful. No money without a trial first, he said! And if all goes well, it'll be well spent. Oh, think of the livery I shall have—all gold trimmings!

PERNILLA: The very fact that he's asking for money proves there's a catch in it. Why should he do that when he can make as much as he wants?

HENRIK: Well, he gave the master a reason, Pernilla.

PERNILLA: Reason? Reason rubbish!! What reason could anybody give?

HENRIK: The reason he gave, my dear, was this: "Alcantara Munki Ezra Mahomet Podolski Cheekimunkicumoffit". It was good enough reason for the master. And what's good enough for the master is good enough for me. That's what I say!

LEONORA: What's all this rigmarole about?

PERNILLA: Yes, what's it all mean?

HENRIK: How should I know, my sweet? Do I understand Arabic?

PERNILLA: You blockhead! If you don't understand, how on earth can you know it was a good reason?

HENRIK: Because the gold-maker said it was. "Spelandisimo Madagascar Hamancino Rencolavet." That's what he said.

PERNILLA: I'm none the wiser.

HENRIK: No more am I, my pretty maid. But what matters is this—he'll get no money till he's delivered the goods. That's the deal they've made. But, look out; here they are! We'd better make ourselves scarce. He'll want to have the gold-maker to himself.

LEONORA: Nothing good can come out of this! I can feel it in my bones. But what does it matter? Ruined tomorrow or the day after—what difference does it make?

They go in as POLIDOR *and* FOX *re-enter from the side door.*

FOX: No, no, no, sir! I beg of you—please! I'll have nothing to do with the actual operation. I want it all to be square and above board; there must be no suspicion of trickery by me. Give it a fair trial yourself, and leave me right out of it. Now, let me see. You put the mercury in the pan as I directed, now, didn't you?

POLIDOR: I did everything exactly as you told me.

FOX: Good, good! Now don't forget to keep it all well on the boil.

POLIDOR: I'll see to that, sir!

FOX: Right! Now here's the secret formula that I told you about. It's in Arabic, you know. You say the words three times while the operation is in progress. I hope you can read them. (*He takes out a piece of paper and reads.*) "Stsimehcla Era Seugor Dna Uoy Era A Loof." Now kneel down, and say that three times after me. (POLIDOR *kneels down and repeats the words three times after* FOX.) That's right! And—er—oh, by the way, don't forget to put the Arabian powder in. Did you do that?

POLIDOR: Arabian powder? What Arabian powder?

FOX: Dear me, didn't I tell you? We musn't forget the Arabian powder, whatever we do! Why, it's as important as anything! It's no good without the Arabian powder.

POLIDOR: But where do I get this—this Arabian powder from? It's the first I've heard of it.

FOX: Oh, no need to worry about that, sir. That's a simple matter. Do you really mean to say you've never heard of Arabian powder? You surprise me, sir. Arabian powder, why, that's the stuff you use for removing stains from clothes. You can get any amount of it for a mark or so. Send your servant round to the market for a bit.

POLIDOR (*to himself*): Arabian powder! Never heard of it. (*Calling.*) Henrik!

HENRIK *appears.*

HENRIK: Master!

POLIDOR: Take this mark and run round to the market for some Arabian powder.

HENRIK: Some what, master?

POLIDOR: Arabian powder. You know, the stuff you use for removing stains from clothes.

HENRIK: Where do I get it from, master?

FOX: You'll find they sell it in the market. (HENRIK *goes off.*)

POLIDOR: Well, fancy that, now! Whoever would have thought that such cheap stuff would be so important? Now are there any other directions we've forgotten?

FOX: No, you have everything now. Here, you'd better keep the slip of paper with the formula, just to remind you. Without that it won't work.

POLIDOR: When do I put the Arabian powder in?

FOX: Any time, so long as the mixture is on the boil. Ah, here's your servant. He's got it, all right. I knew they'd have it in the market. Bound to. (*Enter* HENRIK.)

HENRIK: Here's the Arabian powder, master. And here's the change. I got a cap full for half a mark.

FOX: Right! Now go and put a good handful in the pan.

POLIDOR *and* HENRIK *go in.*

FOX (*rubbing his hands*): Biting nicely! Better let him have another trial, though, just to make sure. It can't go wrong. He'll get ten rix-dollars' worth of gold out of the two handfuls. And then, Brother Andreas, it's over the hills and far away! And if the gentleman can find any more Arabian powder, he'll be a very lucky man. I'm sorry to have to relieve him of his 4,000 rix-dollars, but then, when you come to think of it I shall be doing him a good turn. Teaching him a lesson! Giving him valuable experience! Worth its weight in gold!! Ah, here he comes.

POLIDOR *comes back wild with joy, goes up to Fox, and shakes hands with him.*

POLIDOR: Sir, sir! You've done it! You've proved it! My years of labour have been rewarded—and you have done it. I shall never forget you for this. You've earned your 4,000 rix-dollars. And as much again.

FOX: No, no, sir! I'll accept no more than the sum we agreed on.

POLIDOR: Oh, now I'll teach 'em! This'll be a lesson to 'em, this will! They'll laugh on the other side of their faces now, they will! As for all the la-di-da gentlemen who wouldn't look at me—they'll be on their bended knees, now! Just you see.

FOX: Ah, how right you are, sir! It's the way of the world, and it'll never be any better, I'm afraid.

POLIDOR: I'll show 'em, I will! Just you see if I don't! Oh, I'm going to enjoy this!

FOX: You take my tip, sir. Don't! As my great master Elbofagomar-Fagius would always say, be modest and generous. Now look at me! I could walk about like a prince. You know I could. But that's not my nature. And that's why nobody will ever believe us alchemists—we never put on airs, we're too generous! But we can't help it. And it's the best way in the end.

POLIDOR: I suppose you're right, sir. Well, I'll try to follow your great master's example. Please give him my respects the next time you write.

FOX: I will, sir. You can rely on me, sir.

POLIDOR: And here's my signature. This is Benjamin's authorization to hand you over the money.

FOX: Thank you, sir. But, just a minute. Before I go, why not give it another trial? So as to be quite sure you know how to do it.

POLIDOR: All right, sir. If you'll wait a few minutes, then, I will. (*He goes in.*)

FOX (*chuckling to himself*): Panning out nicely! Nearly time to be off, Andreas, old fellow! (*Enter* LEONORA, *followed by* PERNILLA.)

LEONORA: Oh, sir; what can we do to show our gratitude? At last my husband can make gold. And to think that I never believed in it!

FOX: Madam, my secret's not for sale to everybody. But I took one look at your husband, madam, and I said to myself, " He's a clever man, he is ". And so I made an exception.

PERNILLA: I must kiss your hand, sir! (*She does.*)

FOX: Tut-tut, you do me too great an honour, young lady! My hand's rather dirty. (PERNILLA *kisses his hand again.*) No, no, really; this is too much!

LEONORA: Please accept this ring as a small token of my gratitude and appreciation.

FOX: No, no, no, no, my good lady! Never! I'll accept nothing. You are far too kind. I'll have nothing but the payment I agreed on with your husband.

LEONORA: Do, sir. Just to please me.

PERNILLA: Yes, take it, sir. My mistress will be ever so pleased.

FOX: Very well, then, madam, since you insist. (*He takes it.*)

PERNILLA: I wish I had something to give you. Here, take this locket. It was my mother's.

FOX: No, young lady, I can't take your mother's locket from you.

PERNILLA: Please, sir! I shan't let you go till you do!

FOX: Then I'll take it; and wear it for your sake! I'll send you a gold one in place of it. Ah, here comes the gentleman.

POLIDOR *enters, in the seventh heaven.*

POLIDOR: It's wonderful! You've proved everything you claimed. I got as much gold the second time as I did the first. It's all quite simple. Amazingly simple! And it takes no time at all to do! What can I do to show my gratitude? I hope you'll consider yourself one of the family, and come and go when you like. Won't you stay for a meal now?

FOX: Thank you, sir. Not now; some other time. I shall be here for—well, a little while yet.

POLIDOR: Can't I persuade you to stay now?

FOX: I'm sorry, sir; but I have a very pressing engagement. I must be on my way.

POLIDOR: Then I won't stop you. Benjamin will hand you the money when you show him the authorization I gave you.

FOX: I have no fears on that score, sir. Well, I must be getting off; my friend will be waiting for me. Goodbye—for the present! (*He goes off.*)

POLIDOR:
LEONORA:
PERNILLA: } Goodbye, sir!

POLIDOR: Well, my love, what d'you have to say now, eh? Have I ruined us all by my stupidity, eh? Am I a fool and a fathead, eh?

LEONORA: Husband, I was too hasty. Forgive me.

PERNILLA: Please forgive me, too, master.

POLIDOR: I forgive you both, my dears. But please let this be a lesson to you. Another time—don't argue about things you don't understand. (*Enter* HENRIK.) Hullo, Henrik, where have you sprung from? And what's all the excitement about?

HENRIK: Is it true, master?

POLIDOR: Is what true?

HENRIK: Can you really make gold?

POLIDOR: Yes, Henrik, I can. But who told you?

HENRIK: It's all over the town, master. The first place I heard it was in the tavern round the corner. I couldn't understand what had come over everybody. I was no sooner inside the place than they were all wanting to treat me. Falling over themselves, they were. It's the first time I've ever been treated by anybody in there before! The dog of a landlord would never serve me till my money was on the counter. But now—sends his love to you, he does! Not once—but seven times!!

POLIDOR: There, you see! Just what I expected! You have some bad luck and nobody has any use for you. But when things go well, they're all running after you. But how on earth did it get around so soon?

HENRIK: I expect it was Benjamin, master. Must have told somebody straight away, and then it's all over the town in no time. You should have seen 'em all bowing and scraping to me on the way home! Grand, it was! Master Leander's servant Christopher—him that never used to look at me—he bowed so low he toppled head first in the gutter! Oh, what a mess!! Never looked at him, I didn't. I walked straight past him with my head in the air, just as he used to do with me.

POLIDOR: Hullo, who's this?

HENRIK: Master Leander, I think, master.

POLIDOR: Coming to see me! What did I tell you? He's always snubbed me before.

LEONORA: Turn him away, Henrik. Tell him we're out.

POLIDOR: No, no, my love! Don't let's do that. We'll speak to him. Let's shame him. (*Enter* LEANDER.)

LEANDER: Ah, my dear Polidor! Delighted to see you, I'm sure! De—lighted!! Why, it's months since I saw you! How are you keeping, my dear fellow?

POLIDOR: It isn't for want of calling on you that you haven't seen me, They always said you were out. And if I met you in the street you looked the other way.

LEANDER: But, my dear Polidor, you wrong me; indeed you do! If there's one man in this town I respect, it's you. I swear it, old chap!

POLIDOR: Spare your flattery, sir. It does you no good.

HENRIK: Excuse me, master; I think he is your friend. He's changed. You should have seen him when he heard the news. Bursting with love, he was, master! All of a sudden!

LEANDER: Polidor, I swear! My feelings for you have never changed. I've always thought a lot about you, Polidor, old chap. And let me say this—you can count on my friendship.

POLIDOR: So you say; so you say. However, I must be getting on with my business. I'll bid you Good morning, sir! (*He goes in.*)

LEANDER (*going to* HENRIK *and kissing him*): Please, Henrik! Put a good word in for me with your master, will you? I'm your friend as well as his, you know.

HENRIK: Delighted, I'm sure, sir! Your servant, sir!

He bows, and then they kiss one another on both cheeks. Enter TWO OTHER LACED AND BRAIDED GENTLEMEN, *who bow to* LEONORA *and embrace* HENRIK. LEANDER'S WIFE *comes in, goes up to* LEONORA, *curtsies, and kisses the hem of her apron.*

LEONORA: And what, may I ask, is the meaning of all this fuss?

LEANDER'S WIFE: Fuss, madam? Could there ever be too much fuss over a lady of quality like you?

LEONORA: That's news from you, I must say.

Enter THREE OTHER LADIES, *who go up to* LEONORA, *curtsy, and kiss her apron like the others.*

Well, ladies, I've no time for this nonsense. I'll say Good morning. I have something else to do, and if we go on like this we shall soon have the whole town here.

She goes in. The THREE GENTLEMEN *join their* LADIES, *and bow deeply to* POLIDOR *when he appears at a window. One of them makes such a sweeping bow that he over-balances and falls sprawling on the ground. All six then embrace and kiss* HENRIK, *kiss* PERNILLA'S *hand, and go off.*

PERNILLA: Well, would you believe it, Henrik! Whatever next! Fancy the gentlemen kissing me!—Only my hand, though!

HENRIK: The luckier you! They kissed me on the cheek, they did. Pah!

PERNILLA: Talk about people changing! I can hardly credit it!

HENRIK: Neither can I. To think of all those ladies and gentlemen of quality kissing the hand of a trollop like you!

PERNILLA: And to think of all those ladies and gentlemen of quality kissing the cheek of a bumpkin like you! Really, it was too comical for words! Hullo, more visitors!

TWO OTHER GENTLEMEN *enter with their* LADIES, *and make for the front door.*

HENRIK: Hi, you! Where are *you* going? I'm not sure the master and mistress are in. You'd better stay here till I find out. (*He pushes them away from the door. Enter a young man in black*—A POET.) And who might you be?

POET: A poet, at your service, sir.

HENRIK: Just the man I want! My cat's dead! Do me some lines for its grave, will you?

POET: At your service, sir.

HENRIK (*aside*): Poet! Hang the lot of 'em, I say! (*To* POET.) And what can I do for you?

POET: I've brought this poem that I've written specially for the lady and gentleman of the house.

HENRIK: So that's it! All right. Wait here till they come out. Come on, hurry up! Get over there! (*Pushes him, too, to one side.*) I say, how many verses can you write in a day?

POET: It all depends. It's as the spirit moves me.

HENRIK: Can you do me some verses to rhyme with Henrik Larsen?

POET: That's rather difficult.

HENRIK: Then all I say is, you're not much of a poet. And how is it you've never waited on the master and mistress with your verses before? Tell me that!

POET: I never had the good fortune to know the lady and gentleman before.

HENRIK: You mean you never knew of the lady and gentleman till you heard of their good fortune! If I had my way with you folks I'd hang the lot of you, every man jack of you, for all the good you do. Ah, here comes the master and mistress. They'll soon tell you what they think of you.

POLIDOR *and* LEONORA *appear at the front door, decked out in all their finery.*

POLIDOR: Henrik, take this and get me a dollar's worth of that powder. Then you won't have to be fetching it so often.

HENRIK: Very good master. (*He goes off with the money.*)

POLIDOR (*to the assembled ladies and gentlemen*): And what is your business, my friends?

LADIES and GENTLEMEN:
Your servant, sir!
Your most humble servant!
At your command, good sir!
Your very humble servant!

THE MEN *advance, bowing at every step.* THE LADIES *curtsy to* LEONORA *and kiss the hem of her apron.* THE POET *strikes an attitude, scroll in hand.*

POLIDOR (*to* POET): What on earth have you got there?

POET: A poem in your worship's honour.

POLIDOR: Look you here, you people! Things were going badly with me. My long and unsuccessful experiments had made me neglect my business affairs. You had no use for me then. You scorned my house; you scoffed at me. But now—now my luck has turned. I've discovered the secret of how to make gold; I'm a rich man. And what do I find? You suddenly change your minds about me. You flatterers! If I was the biggest fool in the world you'd call me Solomon. If I was the ugliest I'd be an Apollo. If I was the biggest scoundrel on God's earth you'd be ready to excuse me. And all because of my wealth. When a man has no luck, he has no friends; and when his luck's in, a lot of so-called friends come in with it. Don't think I'm such a simpleton that I can't see through you. You——

HENRIK *comes running in.*

HENRIK: Master, what's the meaning of this? I could get as much as I wanted before. Now there isn't a grain to be got anywhere. Not for its weight in gold, there isn't.

POLIDOR: Eh? What's that you say?

HENRIK: I've been to the market; I've been to all the likely places. And they only laugh in my face. They say there isn't such a thing. They say I've been had!

POLIDOR: Good God! What did you say?

HENRIK: Master, we've been tricked! Swindled; diddled; done in the eye!! There's no such thing as Arabian powder!!

POLIDOR (*with a groan*): My 4,000 rix-dollars!

HENRIK: Hi, what do *you* want? (*Enter the* LANDLORD *of the* "*Pheasant*", *at a run.*) Steady, man! What's come over you? Take it easy, man!

LANDLORD: Oh! Oh! Oh! I wouldn't have minded so much—only it was an heirloom.

PERNILLA: Why, it's the landlord of "The Pheasant"!

LANDLORD: It belonged to my grandmother, it did! Oh, if only her name had been on it!

PERNILLA: Poor fellow! He seems to have gone out of his mind!

LANDLORD: And my spoons. My spoons! And there's sure to be a lot more missing! Oh, my spoons, my spoons!!

HENRIK (*to* LANDLORD, *shaking him*): Hi, Master Landlord! What's come over you? How long have you been like this? The man's mad, I'm sure he is!

LANDLORD: Oh! Oh! Oh!

POLIDOR: What's happened, Master Landlord?

LANDLORD: The stranger—said he was an alchemist—he's run off with all my silver. I thought he was a friend of yours, and so I trusted him. There were two of 'em. The damned, thieving rogues! Just let me get my hands on 'em—I'll——

HENRIK: Two? What sort of a fellow was the other?

LANDLORD: A one-eyed devil!

HENRIK: With a black eye-shade?

LANDLORD: Yes.

HENRIK: And a black fur cap?

LANDLORD: Yes, the——

HENRIK: That's him! I knew it! We've been swindled, all right. That was the fellow that sold me the Arabian powder.

POLIDOR (*groaning*): I've been robbed! Robbed of 4,000 rix-dollars!!

The LADIES *and* GENTLEMEN *prepare to go. In rushes* BENJAMIN.

BENJAMIN: Where's the alchemist? I gave him a jewel with the money!

HENRIK: That just serves you right! You brought him!

BENJAMIN: What—then he was a rogue? Oh, oh, oh; my precious jewel!

POLIDOR: And all I have for my pains and my 4,000 rix-dollars is this bit of paper, with these words that I can't understand—in Arabic.

GENTLEMAN: Arabic, did you say? I know some Arabic. Let me have a look at it. (POLIDOR *hands him the paper.*) Arabic, did you say? Why, this isn't Arabic! It's just a rigmarole!! Hold on, though; what's this? It seems to be the wrong way round. Why, so it is! If you read it backwards the last word spells—Yes—I've got it! Fool!! Bless me, if the whole sentence doesn't make sense—backwards way first! I have it! (*Reading each word slowly backwards.*) " Alchemists—are—rogues—and—you—are—a—fool "!!!

There is a chorus of laughter from the assembled LADIES AND GENTLEMEN, *and they all turn away and walk off. The* POET *turns his back on* POLIDOR, *bows, and walks off also.*

POLIDOR: My 4,000 rix-dollars! My 4,000 rix-dollars!!

LEONORA: And the ring I gave him into the bargain!

PERNILLA: And my locket! And to think I kissed the dirty cheat's filthy hand!!

POLIDOR: Oh, what a fool I've been! Fool!! idiot!! imbecile!!! But it's taught me a lesson—and only just in time. Come, my love! I'll have no more alchemy! And we'll go and live in the country on what little we have left. This has been a lesson I shall never forget.

POLIDOR *takes his* WIFE *by the arm and they go in, followed by* PERNILLA *and* HENRIK, *leaving* BENJAMIN *and the* LANDLORD *to bewail their losses.*

CURTAIN

END OF PLAY

THE HEALING SPRING
(*Kilderejsen*)

A Comedy in a Prologue and One Act

1725

CHARACTERS

LEANDER, in love with Leonora
HENRIK, his servant
LEONORA, in love with Leander
HIERONIMUS, Leonora's father
MAGDELONA, Hieronimus's housekeeper
PERNILLA, maid-servant to Hieronimus
ARV, footman to Hieronimus
NIELS, coachman to Hieronimus
DR. BOMBASTUS
A FOOTMAN

SCENE: A room in the house of Hieronimus

TIME: 1725

The Prologue takes place in a street, but may be played before the curtain, if desired. The curtain is lowered once during the course of the play to indicate the passage of a night, or the illusion may be conveyed by the use of lights.

THE HEALING SPRING

The Prologue takes place in a street, but may be played before the curtain, if desired. LEANDER. *a young man, is pacing up and down impatiently. Enter his servant* HENRIK.

LEANDER: Ah, there you are, Henrik! Still no letters?

HENRIK: No, master. None at all.

LEANDER: I don't know what I shall do if I don't get one soon.

HENRIK: If you ask me, master, you should have gone straight off to see your brother, instead of waiting for his letters.

LEANDER: What makes you say that, Henrik?

HENRIK: Why, the money your father left you would have been yours now, if you had——

LEANDER: There you go! Money, money, money! Love means nothing to you at all!

HENRIK: I wouldn't say that, master. Love's all very well in its way. When Cupid says " Stop! " I'm as ready to stop as anybody. But when Mercury, who puts money in my pocket, says " Go! "—I go double quick!

LEANDER: I wish I could say the same. But it's no use. I'm tied to this place till I've won my Leonora.

HENRIK: And how do you think you're going to win her, as you call it?

LEANDER: Well, there's one little point in my favour, you know, Henrik.

HENRIK: And that is, master?

LEANDER: She loves me.

HENRIK: Much good that will do, when her father keeps her locked up all the time! She might as well love the moon!

LEANDER: Oh come, Henrik, there must be some way out of this! We've got to put our heads together and do something while the old man's away.

HENRIK: Master, it's as simple as A. B. C! Give me the key to the porch door and all the other doors, get somebody to knock the eyes out of that meddlesome footman, who seems to have 'em in the back of his neck—and I'll do the trick for you in a jiffy!

LEANDER: Can't you suggest anything at all? It isn't like you to be stumped for ideas, Henrik.

HENRIK: We're short of time, master. You know as well as I do that her father's coming back tonight—bringing his intended son-in-law with him. Well, I may be pretty good at tricks, but, as I say, we haven't got much time. What's more, we're strangers in these parts. I can only advise you to be patient and wait for the lady's maid. Pernilla's sure to have thought of something. I wonder what can have happened to her! She should be here by now!

LEANDER: What's the time, Henrik?

HENRIK: About four o'clock, master. Not a lot of time left if you're to win the lady before tonight. Ah, here's Pernilla! All smiles! That means she's had an idea. I thought she would.

Enter PERNILLA.

LEANDER: Well, my dear, what news? How's my lady, your mistress? I hope you've found some way of getting her out—or me in? Come along, Pernilla, I can't wait!

PERNILLA: Yes, Master Leander, I have. Hullo, Henrik!

LEANDER: You have?

HENRIK: There! What did I say?

LEANDER: What is it, Pernilla? Tell me quickly!

PERNILLA: And if it works, my mistress and you will be together tonight.

LEANDER: Hurry up and tell me all about it, Pernilla. You're keeping me on tenterhooks!

PERNILLA: Well then, this is the scheme I've arranged with my mistress. She's going to be out of her mind.

LEANDER: What?

PERNILLA: Pretend to be, of course! Whenever anybody speaks to her she'll sing.

HENRIK: That's a queer idea, I must say! Couldn't you have thought of something better than that?

PERNILLA: Now just you be patient a minute, Henrik. It may not be as queer as you think. You see, my mistress is very fond of the opera, and she likes to sing to herself. In fact, it's got to be quite a craze with her and she'll sing away for hours on end. Her father keeps on scolding her for it and says she's silly and stupid. So there couldn't be anything better, really. As a matter of fact, we've already tried it out on Arv, the footman. Oh, you should have seen him! He was scared out of his wits! So now we know it works—and what's more, we shall have to go on with it!

LEANDER: But where do I come in?

PERNILLA: I'll tell you, Master Leander. When my master gets back and finds that his daughter can't speak without singing, he'll be terribly upset, of course. I shall then get him to send for a doctor, the celebrated Dr. Bombastus, who has just arrived here with his son and assistant.

HENRIK: What good will that do? They'll only physic her or something. And then where are we? Just where we were before.

PERNILLA: Ah, now that's where you come in, Henrik!

HENRIK: Me?

PERNILLA: Yes, you. You will be the famous Dr. Bombastus. And your master will be your son. And then you will be able to prescribe the right treatment.

LEANDER: Treatment?

PERNILLA: Yes, you see, tonight is Midsummer Eve—the night people around here go to take the healing waters at our famous spring. All you have to do is to persuade my master to send his sick daughter to the spring and convince him of its magic powers, if he needs any convincing. That shouldn't be so hard to do, as lots of people believe in them, anyway.

LEANDER: But he won't want to go with her?

PERNILLA: Not he! He isn't back from the country yet; and, if I know anything of my master, he won't want to budge for at least another three days. That's what it usually takes him to get over one of his journeys. There's your chance, and you must take it.

HENRIK: And then what?

PERNILLA: As her doctor, you must offer to go with her and see that she takes the waters properly. Then after that Master Leander can decide where to go while he is waiting for my master's consent. Magdelona, the housekeeper, and I would go with you. We need a change as much as my mistress—and for the same reason. We don't get many chances.

HENRIK: But how do I get into the doctor's house?

PERNILLA: You don't. I'll see that the footman comes round to *your* house. All you have to do is to be ready waiting for him—dressed as a doctor. Well, I must go and prepare for my master's return. (*Exit.*)

HENRIK: There, what did I tell you, master? I knew she'd hit on something!

LEANDER: Henrik, we're in luck's way! I'll win my Leonora yet! Come on! (*Exeunt.*)

The Curtain falls, and rises almost immediately on HIERONIMUS'S *drawing-room.* ARV, *the footman, is alone.*

ARV: Well, here's a nice state of affairs! Whatever will the master think? It's enough to drive the old man out of his head! I had the shock of my life! I walk into the room and ask her if it's true the master's coming home tonight, and this is how she answers me. (*He clears his throat and sings in a cracked falsetto voice.*)

Ah, yes, young man; ah, yes, 'tis right!
He's coming tonight; he's coming tonight.

And that's the way she went on, every time I spoke to her. I can't think what's come over her. I wonder if she's bewitched. As for Magdelona and Pernilla, they've done nothing but cry ever since. (*Enter* HIERONIMUS *and* LEONARDO.) Hullo, here's the master—back from his journey, with Master Leonardo! I daren't for the life of me tell him!

HIERONIMUS: My dear Leonardo, the wedding shall take place this week. My mind's made up and I'm not one for wasting time. You've got a nice bit of property there and you seem to have everything ready to receive a wife. So why delay any longer? We'll have it all fixed up for this week. (*Catches sight of* ARV.) Well, Arv, everything all right in the house?

ARV: Well, master . . .

HIERONIMUS: Well what, Arv?

ARV: All right, master, but . . .

HIERONIMUS: But what Arv? Speak up! Has anybody called?

ARV: No, master, but . . .

HIERONIMUS: Nobody been to pay their debts, eh? They have a habit of calling when I'm away!

ARV: No, master, nobody's been, master, but . . .

HIERONIMUS: Damn it all, fellow, what's all this " butting " about?

ARV: Nothing, master! Er—just my way of speaking, master! But . . .

HIERONIMUS: Something has happened, I can see that. I suppose you let my daughter slip through your fingers, eh?

ARV: It's not that, master.

HIERONIMUS: Let her go gadding about the town in my absence, eh? I thought I could trust you, Arv!

ARV: No, master, she hasn't been out while you've been away. I carried out your instructons. It's not that, master. But . . .

HIERONIMUS: The devil take you and your " buts "! What's wrong, then? If it isn't my daughter, what is it?

ARV: Well, master, Mistress Leonora's all right, but she's—she's . . .

HIERONIMUS: What on earth's the matter with her? Confound it, man, out with it!

ARV (*in tears*): Oh, master, I can't tell you. Ask Pernilla and Magdelona.

HIERONIMUS: We'll soon get to the bottom of this. (*He strides over to the door, opens it, and shouts.*) Magdelona! Pernilla! Come in here, both of you!

LEONARDO: Don't upset yourself, Master Hieronimus. The fellow's a fool! I dare say he's only broken something. Or some other minor accident has happened.

HIERONIMUS: There's more to it than that, unless I'm very much mistaken. Ah, here they come! (*Enter* PERNILLA *and* MAGDELONA.) Well, what sort of tricks have you two been up to in my absence?

MAGDELONA: Tricks, master?

HIERONIMUS: What's this I hear about my daughter, Magdelona! (MAGDELONA *only weeps.*) Well, if this wouldn't try the patience of Job! Pernilla, what's this about my daughter? (PERNILLA *bursts into tears.*) Damn it, they're all alike! Arv!

Come here! What's this all about? Out with it, now! (ARV *blubbers with the rest; they make a mournful trio.*) Now listen to me, you three! Unless you want me to warm the backs of all three of you in turn, you'll hurry up and tell me what it's all about! (*Seizing a birch.*) You see this? Right, now which of you's to be first?

MAGDELONA: Oh, master, ask Arv to tell you!

ARV: No, master, ask Pernilla to tell you!
PERNILLA: No, master, ask Magdelona to tell you!

HIERONIMUS: Pernilla, I order you to tell me!

PERNILLA (*tearfully*): All right, master, then I'll tell you. Only please don't get too upset! Last night, between one and two—am I right, Magdelona?

MAGDELONA (*still blubbering*): Nearly two.

PERNILLA: The mistress woke up in a fright. She kept walking up and down, waving her arms about. It was horrible to see her, master. And then, when we asked her what was the matter all she could do was—was . . . (*She breaks down in tears.*)

HIERONIMUS: Well?

PERNILLA (*with a howl*): Sing!!!

HIERONIMUS: What? She—she—she must have been sleep-walking, you foolish girl!

PERNILLA: No, master! She—she's been singing ever since! She's still singing!! She can't speak at all!!!

ARV: That's right, master! I went into her room this morning to ask if you would be coming back tonight. She struck herself on the chest, just as if she was acting in a play, and then started to sing. I haven't got much of a voice, master, but it went something like this. (*Clears his throat and sings as before.*)

Ah, yes, young man; ah, yes, 'tis right!
He's coming tonight; he's coming tonight.

LEONARDO: Good God!

HIERONIMUS: So that's it! That's what comes of this infernal opera-singing! I knew it! I knew it! The crazy girl! Confound the opera! If this goes on we shall be having the whole town singing!

LEONARDO: So far, however, it seems to be only your daughter.

HIERONIMUS: Fetch her here, one of you! We'll soon find out!

PERNILLA: I'll go, master. (*Exit.*)

HIERONIMUS (*as he brandishes the birch*): And if soft words don't produce the explanation, we'll see what else will. The devil take this opera-going and opera-singing! And, Arv, if that singing teacher shows his face here again, have him thrown out, will you? If this wouldn't break a father's heart!

Re-enter PERNILLA, *with* LEONORA. HIERONIMUS *holds the birch behind his back.*

PERNILLA: Here's my mistress.

HIERONIMUS (*gently*): Now, Leonora, my child, what's all this I've been hearing about you? They tell me you've forgotten how to talk, that you can only sing. What's come over you, my child, eh? Frightening your old father out of his wits, you silly girl!

LEONORA (*bursting into song*),

Möchte ich doch, ich doch, ich doch mein treuer Amyntas
Noch ehe ich sterbe wieder sehen!

HIERONIMUS: Great God! German!! This is worse than I thought!!! (*Earnestly.*) Now, look at me, my child. Don't you know me? I'm your father!

LEONORA (*singing*): *Ihr seid mein Vater, ihr seid mein Vater!*

HIERONIMUS (*holding out the birch*): Now look here, Leonora. You see this? Now stop play-acting, or I'll . . .

LEONORA (*singing*): *Gestrenger Vater, gestrenger Vater, halt!*
Das ist ja Tyrannie, das ist ja Gewalt!

LEONARDO: I—I—I feel faint! I must get some fresh air!! Let me know when she recovers!! (*Exit.*)

HIERONIMUS (*with a groan*): There, now Leonardo's gone! The man you were to marry! That's the last straw! I'm finished!! Take her away!!!

PERNILLA: Master, don't you think it would be a good idea to send for a doctor?

HIERONIMUS: Yes, yes, Pernilla! That's right! A doctor!

PERNILLA: Why not send for Dr. Bombastus? The famous new doctor, you know, master. The one that arrived the other day with his son. They say he's a wonderful doctor, master.

HIERONIMUS: Ah, yes, Pernilla, that's it! Better go and fetch him, Arv!

ARV: Dr. Bombastus? Where's he live?

PERNILLA: I know, Arv. His address is . . . (*She mumbles an address in* ARV'S *ear, so that* HIERONIMUS *does not hear.*) Get him to come as soon as he can.

ARV: Right! I'll be back in a few minutes. (*Exit.*)

PERNILLA: I hear he has cured quite a lot of people already, in one way and another.

HIERONIMUS: Yes, I've heard about him.

PERNILLA: They say his son is just as clever as he is.

HIERONIMUS: Who told you all this?

PERNILLA: Mistress Leonora's tutor. Oh, I do hope the doctor can cure her! I'd give anything if he could!

MAGDELONA: Why don't you try to speak to her again, master?

HIERONIMUS: No, Magdelona, I can't bear it! Take her to her room till the doctor comes.

MAGDELONA: Very well, master. Come, dear. (*They go out.*)

HIERONIMUS: And to think that it should come to this! My only child! This was to have been the week of her wedding. Quite a well-set-up young gentleman, too!

PERNILLA: Was that the person who ran away when he saw my mistress was ill?

HIERONIMUS: That was him. It must have been a great shock to find her like that.

PERNILLA: Who is he, master?

HIERONIMUS: A young gentleman from Holstein. He's just come into a lot of money through the death of his father. He'll get as much again, if what they say is right—that his brother has died in foreign parts. He's bought some property near here, and it was all ready for them to move into after the wedding.

PERNILLA: The mistress won't be able to marry him now, will she?

HIERONIMUS: We'll see what the doctor says. By the way, there's another young fellow that's had his eye on her. But he'd better keep his hands off her! Girls of her age are easily carried away. However, I'll see he doesn't come near her! I've taken my precautions.

PERNILLA: So that's why you keep us all shut up like birds in a cage, master?

HIERONIMUS: That's just it. (*As though something dawns on him.*) It couldn't be some mad infatuation for that fellow that has unbalanced her?

PERNILLA: No, master, I don't think so. At least, she's given no sign that she isn't satisfied with your choice. Ah, this must be the doctor!

Enter ARV, *ushering in* HENRIK *and* LEANDER *disguised as Dr. Bombastus and his son. They make exaggerated bows to* HIERONIMUS.

ARV: Dr. Bombastus, master! And the doctor's son!

HIERONIMUS: Ah, there you are, doctor! I apologise for sending for you at such short notice.

HENRIK: Oh, don't mention it, my dear sir, don't mention it! What can I treat you for, sir?

HIERONIMUS: There's nothing wrong with me, I'm pleased to say. It's my poor daughter. She's in a terrible way. It's come on all of a sudden, doctor. I hope you will be able to do something for her.

HENRIK: Of course, of course! It would have to be a very serious complaint, sir, if I couldn't.

HIERONIMUS: I'm glad to hear that, doctor.

HENRIK: Why not let me demonstrate my skill on you, sir?

HIERONIMUS: I'm very grateful, doctor, but I'm glad to say there's nothing wrong with me.

HENRIK: True, true, true! But allow me to make just a small fracture—to show you how quickly I can put it right.

HIERONIMUS: I don't doubt your skill, sir. Everybody here has heard of Dr. Bombastus. I won't trouble you now.

HENRIK: Oh, no trouble, sir! No trouble at all!! My son Theophrastus here will put you right in a trice. Theophrastus!

LEANDER: Yes, Father!

HENRIK: Come, sir, let me make a trial.

HIERONIMUS: No, no, dear doctor! Not now! Another time!

HENRIK: Then let me demonstrate on your footman.

HIERONIMUS: As you wish. Arv, come here to the doctor!

ARV (*stammering with fright*): Oh—oh!——

HIERONIMUS: Now, don't be foolish! He'll cure you right away.

ARV: Oh—oh!

HENRIK: Come here, my boy! It won't take more than a minute!

ARV: Oh—oh—!!

HENRIK: I see he doesn't want to. Never mind! But what ails your daughter?

HIERONIMUS: I think her mind must be unbalanced.

HENRIK: In what way, sir?

HIERONIMUS: She doesn't seem to be able to talk. She sings when we speak to her.

HENRIK: Ah, yes, yes, yes! I know the complaint. *Perisangia*, without a doubt, sir! Let me feel her pulse. (*To* PERNILLA.) How long have you been like this, my dear? Don't worry! We'll soon have you right!

PERNILLA: I thank you kindly, doctor! There's nothing wrong with me!

HIERONIMUS: No, doctor, that's my maid. Arv, call Mistress Leonora!

ARV: Very good, master! (*Exit.*)

HENRIK: Oh, of course, of course! How foolish of me!

He chucks PERNILLA *under the chin and, when he can do so without being observed by* HIERONIMUS, *exchanges facetious asides with her.* ARV *returns with* LEONORA.

HIERONIMUS: This is my daughter.

HENRIK: Ah yes, I see. I knew it as soon as I saw her! *Perisangia*—there's no doubt about it!!

LEANDER *exchanges meaningful looks with* LEONORA, *and throughout this scene, when unobserved, they too carry on some by-play of their own.*

HENRIK: What do *you* think, Theophrastus?

LEANDER: Er—Ah, yes, Father! Er—observe the nose! See this *circumflex*, this *dolus malus*!!

HENRIK: Yes, yes, yes, my son! Dear, dear, dear!! That *circumflex* alone shows it to be *perisangia*! Feel her pulse, my son.

LEANDER (*whispering to* LEONORA): We'll have you out tonight!

HIERONIMUS (*to* HENRIK): Won't you put your hat down,

doctor? It's in your way. Here, Arv, come and take the doctor's hat!

ARV (*too scared*): Oh—oh——!

HIERONIMUS: God bless me, the lad must be off his head! Here, come and take the doctor's hat, I say!

ARV: Oh—oh——!

HENRIK: He seems to be afraid of me. I may as well put it on. By your leave, my good lady! Now let me feel that pulse! Ah, yes, it's beat is quite *perisangialeter*! Feel again, my son, and tell me what you think.

LEANDER (*taking* LEONORA's *hand and gazing into her eyes*): Father, I think this is more than a *perisangia*! This must be a—an *archisangia*!!

HENRIK: Let me feel: My son, I believe you are right! The pulse certainly has an *archisangial* beat!! But don't you worry, my good lady! My son will soon cure you!

LEANDER: Put yourself in my hands, my dear lady, and I'll soon have you all right.

LEONORA (*bursting into song*):

Oh, you will set me free,
For you alone allure me!
Ah, you my doctor be,
For you alone can cure me!

HIERONIMUS: Oh, my heart bleeds for her! But I'm glad she has confidence in the doctor!

PERNILLA: Don't you worry, master! He'll soon cure her.

HENRIK: It's always a great help when a doctor has his patient's confidence.

LEONORA (*singing*):

I gaze into your eyes,
And happy am again, sir!
Then vanish all my sighs;
Then gone is all my pain, sir!

Oh, you will set me free,
For you alone allure me!
Ah, you my doctor be,
For you alone can cure me!

HIERONIMUS: Sounds a bit strong, Pernilla!

PERNILLA: I suppose it's from one of these operas again, master.

HIERONIMUS: She's stopped singing in German, anyway! There's some improvement already, doctor!

LEANDER: Sir, we'll have her cured in no time! I'll stake my medical reputation on it! Within two days, my dear lady, you'll be perfectly all right!

LEONORA:
Oh, you will set me free,
For you alone allure me!
Ah, you my doctor be,
For you alone can cure me!

HENRIK: And now, sir, I must confer with my son about the treatment. Theophrastus, *quid tibi videtur*? Er—*post molestam senectutem nos habetit humus.*

LEANDER: Er—*nomen pronomen verbum participium supimum præpositio conjunctio.*

HENRIK: *Adjectivum et substantivum genere numero et pluraliter.*

LEANDER: Er—*rusticus in via*—er—*si non vis credere, gusta.*

HENRIK: *Gratias quam maximam ago quia quoniam quando.*

LEANDER: *Tunc tua res agitur, paries proximus ardet.*

They have been working themselves up and are by this time quite excited.

HENRIK: *Alpha beta gamma delta ypselon ponto basta.*

LEANDER: *Ad adversus adversum pro contra extra supra palam archipodialiter tenus.*

ARV, *who has edged away whenever either of the " doctors " has approached him, has now lost his nervousness and is hopping gleefully around them, hoping for a fight.*

ARV: That's it! You tell him!! Just let him have it!!! Give him one on the jaw!!! Break one or two bones and show us how you put 'em together again!!!

HENRIK: *Omnia conando docilis solertia vincit.*

LEANDER: *Pes aries paries plames sum limite stipes.*

HENRIK: *Quisquis amat ranam, ranam putat esse Dianem. Quando duo substantium concurrent, alterum erat infinitivi.*

LEANDER: *Tityre; To patula recubans solertia vincit.*

HENRIK: Good, good, my son! I quite agree with you. In fact, I agreed with you from the first! I just wanted to test your principles! As it happens, your daughter has been taken ill at a very convenient time, Master Hieronimus.

HIERONIMUS: Convenient, you say? Damned inconvenient, I'd call it! Her wedding has been fixed for this week.

LEANDER: You misunderstand, sir. My father means it is convenient because tonight happens to be Midsummer Eve.

HIERONIMUS: What on earth has that got to do with it?

LEANDER: Why, the spring, sir!

HIERONIMUS: Spring?

LEANDER: Yes, spring, sir. Don't you see, sir? Your daughter must drink the waters.

HIERONIMUS: What good will that do her?

LEANDER: Ah, sir, there's more healing in those waters than you might think!

HENRIK: Mind you, they have to be taken in the right way and at the right time, and after a few preliminary preparations.

LEANDER: There's a little powder which must be taken first.

HIERONIMUS: Well, then, I suppose she had better make the journey, if you say so.

HENRIK: It's the one thing that can cure her, sir.

HIERONIMUS: But I don't see how I can go tonight. I've only just got back from another journey.

LEANDER: Tonight is the only night, sir.

HIERONIMUS: I suppose you couldn't go with her, doctor? Just to see she is all right!

HENRIK: I'm a busy man, sir, as you can imagine. However, either I or my son will accompany your daughter. Somebody must go to administer the preliminary medicine, in any case.

HIERONIMUS: But please see that she speaks to nobody on the way. There have been one or two young bucks after her, and I don't want to take any chances.

HENRIK: Very well, sir. Your daughter will be in safe hands.

HIERONIMUS: I suppose you'll have to be starting soon. Pernilla and Magdelona, you'd better help your mistress to get ready. And you go with her, if you like. Arv, tell Niels to get the carriage out and harness the horses! I'll have a word with him later, before he goes. (*They go off to do as they are bidden.*) Meanwhile, I hope you two gentlemen will take a little refreshment.

It will be a tiring journey. Would you come this way, please! As I was saying, doctor . . .

As they go out together the curtain is lowered to indicate the passage of a night. After a brief pause it rises again on an empty stage. Enter HIERONIMUS.

HIERONIMUS: Arv! Arv! Where are you?

ARV (*off-stage*): Coming, master! (*He enters from the other side, stretching himself and yawning.*) Oh!! What—what have we to get up in the middle of the night for?

HIERONIMUS: Night? Night with the sun shining?

ARV: You can't go by the sun at midsummer, master. It has to make up for lost time in winter! When we've only candle-light to work by! Oh!! (*Yawns again.*) Oh!!

HIERONIMUS: Well, I'll admit it's a bit early. But I was anxious to hear about that daughter of mine. What time did they get back?

ARV: Get back, Master? Nobody's back yet.

HIERONIMUS: What! You don't mean to tell me she's been out all night? There would have been plenty of time to take the waters and get home again before midnight. They don't cure people at night.

ARV: All depends on the complaint, master! Some complaints are best cured at night! Anyway, the doctor knows best.

HIERONIMUS: All the same, I'd be happier in my mind if she was here. It looks as if I shall have to set out and find her. If only I wasn't so damned tired after that last journey! You'd better get ready to go with me, Arv. (*There is a knock at the door.*) See who that it, will you?

ARV *opens the door to* HENRIK.

ARV: The doctor!

HENRIK: I'd like a word with your master. Is he in?

ARV: Oh, doctor, promise not to touch me!

HENRIK: That's all right, my boy. I'm not going to hurt you. Where's your master?

ARV (*calling*): It's the doctor back, master!

HIERONIMUS: Show him in, then! Come in, doctor! I'm delighted to see you I was feeling a bit worried about my daughter not being back. In fact, I was just setting out to look for her.

HENRIK: There's no need, sir. Your daughter is in safe hands. She is already cured and—er—may be home tonight. I've just had a note from my son. Here it is. (*Pulls out a paper and reads it.*) " *Spelandissimo corivendum doctus doctior doctissimus. . . .*" Ah, but I suppose you don't understand Latin, sir.

HIERONIMUS: No, doctor.

HENRIK: Then I'll translate it. This is what it says. " Most learned and celebrated Doctor! My esteemed dear Father! I write to inform you of the progress I have made in curing the patient. As we agreed, I prescribed two powders to be taken by the lady, one before drinking the waters, the other after. The first powder, you will recall, was the tincture called . . ."

HIERONIMUS: Tincture! That's not a powder!

HENRIK: That is where you are mistaken, sir. The authorities agree that it is. I proceed: " The first powder is the tincture called *silliasinine*. No sooner had the patient taken this powder than she grew worse. In fact, she sang without stopping. I then caused her to drink the water, three and one-thirteenth quarts, the amount prescribed by Hippocrates. For, as Hippocrates says, *Helenu omikron pi ro sigma* . . ."

HIERONIMUS: We'll skip what Hippocrates says.

HENRIK: Very well! Where was I? Ah, yes. " I then caused her to drink the waters "—er—etc. " She quickly began to recover, and as soon as she had finished drinking she put her arms round me and said, without singing: " Ah, dear doctor! ' And a heavy load fell from my heart. Since then she has only sung two or three times, and I hope that when I have given her the *essentia scholastica*, about noon today, she will be fully recovered and will be able to go home. Perhaps this evening. Written in great haste by your faithful and affectionate son, Theophrastus. *Manu mea propria.*"

HIERONIMUS: Oh, my dear doctor, this is good news indeed! I feel a lot easier in my mind now. How can I express my thanks? Let me have your bill, doctor!

HENRIK: Oh, that can wait, sir! No hurry about that!

There is another knock at the door.

HIERONIMUS: See who that is, Arv!

ARV: Right, master! (*He opens the door to* FOOTMAN,) Well?

FOOTMAN: Which gentleman is Master Hieronimus?

HIERONIMUS: Here, my man! What's your errand?

FOOTMAN: I have a message from my master, Dr. Bombastus. He's outside and wishes to speak to you.

HIERONIMUS: Eh? What! But—but your master's here! Look!

FOOTMAN: Beggin' your pardon, sir, but my master's outside.

HIERONIMUS: What on earth's the meaning of this? Well, tell him to come in!

HENRIK (*aside*): Ugh! Here's a pretty kettle of fish! But where there's life, there's hope!! My word should be as good as his!!!

Enter BOMBASTUS.

BOMBASTUS: Good morning, sir! I must apologize for calling so early! But I have just heard that your daughter has been taken seriously ill, and so I hastened to offer my assistance.

HIERONIMUS: What's your name, sir?

BOMBASTUS: Bombastus, sir. The well-known Dr. Bombastus, recently arrived in this town, at your service!

HIERONIMUS: It can't be!

BOMBASTUS: What was that you said, sir?

HIERONIMUS: My daughter may have been wandering in her mind, but I'm pretty certain I'm not! You don't mean to say there are two Dr. Bombastus's?

BOMBASTUS: No, only one, and I am the man.

HENRIK: It's a lie! I'm Dr. Bombastus!!

BOMBASTUS: What? How dare you, sir! Who are *you*?

HENRIK: I've told you! Dr. Bombastus! How dare you use my name!

BOMBASTUS: The insolence of the fellow! What do you mean by using my name?

HENRIK: Who gave *you* permission to call yourself Dr. Bombastus? That's my name!

BOMBASTUS: You Bombastus! The devil you are!

HENRIK: The devil yourself! You're not Bombastus!

HIERONIMUS: This is rich! I don't know *where* I am now!!

ARV: I wish I was somewhere else! Too many doctors about for my liking!!

BOMBASTUS: Imagine! To be told I'm not myself!

HENRIK: Fancy the man daring to deny me to my face!

BOMBASTUS: The limit! I'm . . .

HENRIK: You're not Dr. Bombastus!

BOMBASTUS: By Apollo, I swear I am!

HENRIK: And by Cornelius Nepos, I swear I am!

BOMBASTUS: Who on earth is *he*?

HENRIK: He's as good as Apollo any day!

BOMBASTUS: You don't know what you're talking about! Apollo is the god of medicine!

HENRIK: All right! Cornelius Nepos is the god of springs!

BOMBASTUS (*to* HIERONIMUS): Sir, this fellow is no doctor. I fear you have been tricked.

HENRIK: Master Hieronimus, that's the fellow who's trying to trick you! He knows nothing about medicine!

BOMBASTUS: Very well! I'll prove your ignorance!

HENRIK: I'll prove yours!!

BOMBASTUS: Answer me this simple question. What does *circulatio sanguinis* mean?

HENRIK: Chicken-pox!

BOMBASTUS: A pox on your chicken-pox!

HENRIK: All right, then! Now you answer this simple question. What does *essentia scholastica* mean?

BOMBASTUS: There's no such thing in medicine.

HENRIK: There you are! I told you so! He's proved his ignorance! Master Hieronimus, I'm wasting my time arguing with such a fellow! He's never heard of *essentia scholastica*!!

HIERONIMUS: Does that show he's not a doctor?

HENRIK: By Jove, that's the essence my son has cured your daughter with!

HIERONIMUS: You're quite right! He must be an impostor, then!

BOMBASTUS: You don't mean to say that you take his word before mine? I shall proceed to expose him! (*To* HENRIK.) Listen here, fellow! *Quid tibi videtur de sympathia*?

HENRIK: *Intentum particularis sub rosa corivendum clemmabassiando!!*

ARV: He's giving him it now!

BOMBASTUS: What's that gibberish?

HENRIK: Arabic, you fool!

BOMBASTUS: What? You dare to call me a fool? You insolent impostor, you!! I'll show you, you rogue!! You villain!!!

They fly at each other's throats, to ARV'S *intense delight. In the scuffle* BOMBASTUS *pulls off* HENRIK'S *coat, revealing the livery underneath.*

ARV: Oh, look, master! Look!! Why, it's the servant of the stranger who's been running after Mistress Leonora!!!

HIERONIMUS (*grimly*): A pretty business, this is! Lock the door, Arv! Don't let him get out! Oh, what a fatheaded fool I've been! I might have known!! Now I see the " doctor " I can guess who his " son " is!! (*To* BOMBASTUS.) Doctor, I've been made a fool of!

BOMBASTUS: So I perceive. But what is behind all this?

HIERONIMUS (*to* HENRIK): Now explain everything, you rogue! The more you try to hide, the worse it'll be for you!!

HENRIK: I'll tell you everything, sir!

HIERONIMUS: I want to know the truth!

HENRIK: The truth is, I was a doctor and now I'm only a lackey!

HIERONIMUS: So you think you can go on making a fool of me, do you? (*Seizing* HENRIK *by the throat.*) I'll teach you to mock at me, you rogue! You dog, I'll choke the life out of you!!

HENRIK: Oh, spare me, sir! I'll confess everything! It—it was all your maid's idea!

HIERONIMUS: What was?

HENRIK: The idea that your daughter should pretend to be out of her mind. And it was her idea that I should pretend to be a doctor and get you to send your daughter to the healing spring to be cured.

HIERONIMUS: And who's the fellow that pretended to be your son and assistant, and has gone off with my daughter?

HENRIK: Why, my master, of course! Who else do you think?

HIERONIMUS (*with a groan*): I knew it! I knew it! This is the limit! And where are they now, you dog?

HENRIK: They went off from the spring together.

HIERONIMUS: Just as I expected! And to think that my coachman let them go! Niels!! A man I trusted completely!!

HENRIK: The coachman's innocent, sir. As a matter of fact, I think he's still looking for them. They escaped from him in a farm cart.

There is a knock at the door.

HIERONIMUS: See who it is this time, Arv!

ARV *opens the door.*

ARV: It's Niels, master! And Master Leonardo!

HIERONIMUS: Niels! So you've come! Where have you been all this time?

Enter NIELS. LEONARDO *steps in unobserved by* HIERONIMUS.

NIELS: Good morning, master! Oh, what a night!! What a night!!!

HIERONIMUS: What happened, Niels? Where's my daughter?

NIELS: Women! Give me horses any day!! I know how to handle them!! But your women, master!! There's no knowing what they're going to do next!! What a night!!! What a night!!!

HIERONIMUS: Tell me what happened, Niels.

NIELS: What happened, master? Well, when we got to the spring they gave me a few drinks. And it wasn't spring water, neither! However, after a bit I managed to get up and have a walk round, just to see what was going off, like, and little thinking but what everything was all right. But just as the fun's at its best and I'm beginning to enjoy myself, somebody comes and tells me the young lady has gone off with her two women and a young man, full gallop in a farm cart. Well, I runs back to our carriage and all I finds is a doctor's cloak, from which I reckons that it must 'ave been a disguise. So, taking a couple o' strong fellows with me, I rides after 'em, till the horses are fit to drop. At the first inn on the road I finds 'em. My, master, but that doctor's a terror! I've got bruises all over me! Oh, my head!! To say nothing o' my back and my axles!!! However, all's well that ends well, as they say! We got the better of 'em in the end, and I've brought the whole bag o' tricks with me back in the carriage, doctor and all!

HIERONIMUS: Well done, Niels! And where are they now?

NIELS: All safely locked up in the stable, with one of the stable hands to guard the door.

HIERONIMUS (*seeing* LEONARDO): Hullo, son-in-law! Back again? Have you been here long?

LEONARDO: Long enough to hear all I wanted to hear. I suppose, coachman, the young lady has stopped singing now?

NIELS: You can bet your boots on that, sir! She's having a nice good cry now!

HIERONIMUS: The singing was only a trick. This fellow here has confessed to all that! Right, thank you Niels! You've done a good job! I'll bear it in mind! Now send Magdelona in, would you? We'll hear her side of the story first.

NIELS: Very good, master!

HIERONIMUS: And you might tell her, Niels, that we've got a real doctor here who can read people's thoughts!

NIELS (*aside*): That's a good one! I warrant she'll have one or two things of her own to confess! (*Exit.*)

HIERONIMUS: And now, Leonardo, as soon as I've thrashed Pernilla—and hanged this rogue here—we'll make arrangements for the wedding.

LEONARDO: With all due respect to yourself, Master Hieronimus, I submit that you can hardly expect me to marry a woman who has eloped with another man. It would scarcely be decent.

HIERONIMUS: No, I suppose not. I see what you mean. I can hardly blame you for not wanting her after this! (*Enter* MAGDELONA.) Ah, here's the first culprit! So there you are, Magdelona! You—you bawd!! I regard you, as the oldest, as the worst of the whole pack! You ought to know better! Let me tell you right away that I haven't brought you in here for information. I already know all there is to be known. I want your confession.

MAGDELONA (*on her knees*): Oh, Master Hieronimus, don't punish me! I'll promise to confess everything! Both about myself and about my mistress!

HIERONIMUS (*aside*): Herself! There may be more in this than I thought! (*To* MAGDELONA.) Right, then confess your own sins first. And don't try to hide anything. The doctor here can tell.

MAGDELONA: I don't mind telling you, master, because I've been deceived.

HIERONIMUS: Deceived? Who by?

MAGDELONA: My lover, master. At least that's what he pretended to be. And I'm sure I've been very good to him. I've given him all sorts.

HIERONIMUS: Yes, I've heard all about that from the doctor. But tell me what you took from the house to give him.

MAGDELONA: Only a pound of sugar now and then, master. A bottle of wine, and a few things like that.

HIERONIMUS: Go on, go on! What about the money you took?

MAGDELONA: Money, master? What money?

HIERONIMUS: Now don't force me to ask the doctor to tell. It'll be all the worse for you if I have to!

MAGDELONA (*appealing to* BOMBASTUS): Oh, Master Doctor, don't tell lies against me! If I'd given him any money I'd have confessed.

HIERONIMUS: All right, then! We'll leave it at that!

MAGDELONA: I'd arranged to meet him at the spring. But when I got there I found the wretch carrying on with another woman. Am I telling the truth, doctor?

BOMBASTUS: Yes, yes; that's quite right!

HIERONIMUS: Now tell us something about my daughter's affair.

MAGDELONA: Pernilla knows more about that than I do, master. The spring was her idea.

HIERONIMUS: All right! Fetch her in, Arv!

ARV: Very good, master! (*Exit.*)

HIERONIMUS: First of all, we'll find out what she was doing there. I'll wager she had some business of her own!

Re-enter ARV *with* PERNILLA, *who falls on her knees before* HIERONIMUS.

ARV: Here she is, master.

PERNILLA: Oh, master, forgive me! I only did it out of love for my mistress! I'll confess everything, master!

HIERONIMUS: The doctor here has already told me about you. What have you got to say for yourself? Love-making on the sly, eh?

PERNILLA: I confess! It was all my idea! I did it to help my mistress and her lover. They have both been very good to me.

HIERONIMUS: We know all that! But what about this love affair of your own? Eh?

PERNILLA: There isn't one!

HIERONIMUS: Master Doctor, let's hear the story from you!

BOMBASTUS: Well—er—it's like this . . .

PERNILLA: No! I'll tell it myself!!! I arranged to meet a young gentleman at the spring. He's a nice young gentleman, and why shouldn't I do him a small favour now and then? He'll stick up for me if you punish me, master!

HIERONIMUS: That'll do! That'll do! This sacred spring!!! These holy waters!!! It's nothing but an excuse for whoring!!! You women are all alike. Anyone would think I never looked after you!

BOMBASTUS: If every servant-girl who went to the spring last night were cross-examined, we should have a pretty collection of tales, I'm thinking!

HIERONIMUS: That's why I believe in keeping them at home.

BOMBASTUS: But can't you see that that only makes them worse! It isn't a bit of use trying to cage them up! Better to give them a reasonable amount of freedom!

HIERONIMUS: I wouldn't mind if it was only the maids! But my daughter!! My daughter going off on these—these whoring expeditions!!!

PERNILLA: She didn't, master! She's in love with a nice young gentleman who wants to marry her.

HIERONIMUS: I'll see him hanged first! The knave!! One of you fetch my daughter!!

ARV: I'll go, master. (*Exit.*)

BOMBASTUS: Now don't be too severe with her. You know what young people are! Remember you were once in love yourself, sir!

HIERONIMUS: Love! This isn't love!! This is lechery!! She feigns madness so as to be able to elope with a—a vagabond!

BOMBASTUS: Ah, here she comes!

Re-enter ARV *with* LEONORA *who falls on her knees, weeping.*

ARV: Here she is, master.

LEONORA (*weeping*): My dearest father!

HIERONIMUS: Father! I'll be no father to—to a—a night-bird!!

Fathers of women like you are entitled to thrash them and turn them out!!!

LEONORA: Father, I'm sorry! I never meant to offend you! I was only thoughtless!

HIERONIMUS: Thoughtless! Say wicked!! You make a fool of your old father by pretending to be mad and then you run off with a knave and a vagabond!! Do you want me to be a laughing-stock for the rest of my life?

LEONORA: He's no knave and no vagabond, Father. He's a handsome gentleman with means of his own, and he comes off as good a family as I do.

HIERONIMUS: Gentleman! His actions show him to be one, don't they? But I've no doubt he's good enough for a slut like you! I've a good mind to have you locked up for the rest of your life! Not that you're too nice for him! Oh, no!! But because that's what you deserve, you—you trollop!!! (LEONORA *is sobbing*.) Yes, that's it! Weep! Weep the way you used to sing! You'll not deceive me any more! Look, here's the gentleman you were to have been married to! But he's changed his mind now, and no wonder! Who would want to marry a strumpet like you? As for you other hussies, I'll have you whipped within an inch of your lives! And you, Master self-made Doctor, you've got a hanging coming to you! Now for the master of ceremonies himself! Fetch the rascal in, somebody! (*Exit* ARV.) We'll soon settle his hash! He'll rue the day he set eyes on *my* daughter!

Re-enter ARV, *with* LEANDER.

ARV: Here he is, master.

HIERONIMUS (*mocking*): Your servant, sir! I see from your dress that you have decided to abandon the practice of medicine. I must thank you for the trouble you took over my daughter. I gather that your services were not tendered for nothing.

LEANDER: Master Hieronimus, I do not doubt that you take me for a scoundrel, but I can assure you that my intentions were perfectly honourable and that I have done nothing that any honourable man would not have done in my place. I love your daughter.

HIERONIMUS: Rubbish! Shall I remind you of what the law has

to say about thieves who sneak into other men's houses and abscond with their daughters? Answer me, sir!

LEANDER: I swear to you that I am an honest man! And, moreover, I come of a good family and can prove it.

LEONARDO: What's this I hear? Surely I know that voice? And that face? No, no, it can't be! But—Yes, by Heaven, it is! Leander!! My brother!!!

LEANDER: What? Who—? Leonardo!! Brother!!! After all these years!!! Leonardo!!! *(They embrace.)*

LEONARDO: And to think that you, Leonardo, were my rival!! How long have you been in this place?

LEANDER: On the receipt of your letter I left Madrid immediately for Holland. There I took ship for home, arrived here three weeks ago, and have been detained here ever since by this charming lady, with whom I fell in love at first sight and who is the innocent cause of all these adventures.

LEONARDO: Brother, your share of Father's estate is waiting for you. And as for my intended bride, I gladly yield her to you, since I see that she loves you and you love her!

HIERONIMUS: Wha—at? Brother, you say?

The three women have risen to their feet. HENRIK *hugs himself.*

HENRIK (*jubilant*): No hanging this time, unless I'm very much mistaken!

PERNILLA: Or whipping, either!

HIERONIMUS (*quite bewildered*): This—this isn't just another trick to deceive me?

LEONARDO: No, Master Hieronimus. This is no trick. Leander is my brother, my only brother. It's so long since I heard from him that I had really given him up for dead, and had claimed his fortune. But I never renounced anything with greater pleasure than I now renounce that.

HIERONIMUS: And did I understand you to say that you renounced my daughter's hand as well?

LEONARDO: Master Hieronimus, I could never have the heart to separate two people who seem so closely attached to each other—not even if they were both strangers! Of course I renounce your daughter's hand! But on one condition! That you will forgive them all!!

HIERONIMUS: With all my heart! Leonora, my dear, you shall be my daughter again! Leander, I'll have you for my son-in-law! Magdelona and Pernilla, you can forget the thrashings! And as for you, fellow (*to* HENRIK), I'm not going to hang anybody! We're going to have a grand reunion and betrothal celebration!! Thank heaven that what had every appearance of ending in tragedy has suddenly turned out to be a comedy!!!

HENRIK: Ladies and gentlemen! I'm sure you will agree that we have proved the magic power of our healing spring. This good lady is not the first to be cured by it, and I don't think she'll be the last. What do *you* say, Pernilla?

CURTAIN

END OF PLAY

THE DRAMA LIBRARY

NOAH — ANDRÉ OBEY
Introduction by Michel Saint-Denis — 4*s.* 6*d.*

THE IMPORTANCE OF BEING EARNEST — OSCAR WILDE
Introduction by Sir John Gielgud — 4*s.* 0*d.*

TIME AND THE CONWAYS — J. B. PRIESTLEY
Introduction by Irene Hentschel — 3*s.* 6*d.*

TEN DIMINUTIVE DRAMAS — MAURICE BARING
Introduction by Sir Desmond MacCarthy — 4*s.* 6*d.*

HASSAN — J. E. FLECKER
Introduction by Basil Dean — 4*s.* 0*d.*

THE GOVERNMENT INSPECTOR — NIKOLAI GOGOL
English Text by D. J. Campbell
Introduction by Janko Lavrin — 4*s.* 6*d.*

A MONTH IN THE COUNTRY — IVAN TURGENEV
English Text by Emlyn Williams
Introduction by Michael Redgrave — 4*s.* 6*d.*

CYRANO DE BERGERAC — EDMOND ROSTAND
English Text by Brian Hooker — 6*s.* 0*d.*

AN ENEMY OF THE PEOPLE — HENRIK IBSEN
Introduction by Ivor Brown — 5*s.* 0*d.*

THREE MEDIEVAL PLAYS — Edited: JOHN ALLEN
EVERYMAN: COVENTRY NATIVITY PLAY: MASTER PIERRE PATHELIN — 5*s* 0*d.*

THE SNOW QUEEN — SURIA MAGITO AND RUDOLF WEIL
Introduction by Michel Saint-Denis — 4*s.* 6*d.*

THE SATIRE OF THE THREE ESTATES — SIR DAVID LINDSAY
Edinburgh Festival Version by Robert Kemp
Introduction by Tyrone Guthrie — 3*s.* 6*d.*

TAMBURLAINE THE GREAT — CHRISTOPHER MARLOWE
Acting version prepared and introduced by Tyrone Guthrie and Donald Wolfit — 4*s.* 6*d.*

EMMANUEL — JAMES FORSYTH
A Nativity Play — 3*s.* 6*d.*

LIKE STARS APPEARING — VISCOUNT DUNCANNON
Introduction by E. Martin Browne — 5*s.* 0*d.*

THE MAKERS OF VIOLENCE — ROBERT GITTINGS
The Canterbury Festival Play, 1951 — 4*s.* 0*d.*

HIS EMINENCE OF ENGLAND — HUGH ROSS WILLIAMSON
The Canterbury Fesitval Play, 1953 — 4*s.* 6*d.*

TWO SAINTS' PLAYS — 4*s.* 6*d.*
ST. CHAD OF THE SEVEN WELLS — LEO LEHMAN
MAN'S ESTATE — ROBERT GITTINGS

THE PLAYER KING — CHRISTOPHER HASSALL — 6*s.* 0*d.*

WILL SHAKESPEARE — CLEMENCE DANE
Introduction by Basil Dean — 6*s.* 0*d.*

SPRING, 1600 — EMLYN WILLIAMS — 4*s.* 6*d.*

TRESPASS — EMLYN WILLIAMS — 5*s.* 0*d.*

CAVALCADE — NOËL COWARD
Introduction by the Author — 4*s.* 6*d.*

LETTER FROM PARIS — DODIE SMITH
Based on Henry James' *The Reverberator* — 6*s.* 0*d.*

CARRINGTON, V.C. — DOROTHY AND CAMPBELL CHRISTIE
Introduction by Alec Clunes — 8*s.* 6*d.*

SIX CHARACTERS IN SEARCH OF AN AUTHOR — LUIGI PIRANDELLO
English Text and Introduction by Frederick May — 5*s.* 0*d.*

FOUR ONE-ACT PLAYS — 7*s.* 6*d.*
BIRTHDAY MESSAGE — Tyrone Guthrie
THE ASSET — Robert Kemp
GOSSIPS — John Allen
THROUGH A GLASS, LIGHTLY — Robert Gittings